THE ANTI-CAPITALISTIC MENTALITY

The Anti-capitalistic Mentality

Ludwig von Mises

KÍRION PRESS

FLORIDA
2023

THE ANTI-CAPITALISTIC MENTALITY
Ludwig von Mises

Kirion Press
Florida, 2023

Cover design by Laura Barreto

ISBN 978-1-959904-02-1

CONTENTS

Introduction

The substitution of laissez-faire capitalism for the precapitalistic methods of economic management has multiplied population figures and raised in an unprecedented way the average standard of living. A nation is the more prosperous today the less it has tried to put obstacles in the way of the spirit of free enterprise and private initiative. The people of the United States are more prosperous than the inhabitants of all other countries because their government embarked later than the governments in other parts of the world upon the policy of obstructing business. Nonetheless many people, and especially intellectuals, passionately loathe capitalism. As they see it, this ghastly mode of society's economic organization has brought about nothing but mischief and misery. Men were once happy and prosperous in the good old days preceding the "Industrial Revolution." Now under capitalism the immense majority are starving paupers ruthlessly exploited by rugged individualists. For these scoundrels nothing counts but their moneyed interests. They do not produce good and really useful things, but only what will yield the highest profits. They poison bodies with alcoholic beverages and tobacco, and souls and minds with tabloids, lascivious books and silly moving pictures. The "ideological superstructure" of capitalism is a literature of decay and degradation, the burlesque show and the art of strip-tease, the Hollywood pictures and the detective stories.

The bias and bigotry of public opinion manifests itself most clearly in the fact that it attaches the epithet "capitalistic" exclusively to things abominable, never to those of which everybody approves. How can any good come from capitalism! What is valuable has been produced in spite of capitalism, but the bad things are excrescences of capitalism.

It is the task of this essay to analyze this anti-capitalistic bias and to disclose its roots and its consequences.

I.
The Social Characteristics of Capitalism and the Psychological Causes of Its Vilification

1. The Sovereign Consumer

The characteristic feature of modern capitalism is mass production of goods destined for consumption by the masses. The result is a tendency towards a continuous improvement in the average standard of living, a progressing enrichment of the many. Capitalism deproletarianizes the "common man" and elevates him to the rank of a "bourgeois."

On the market of a capitalistic society the common man is the sovereign consumer whose buying or abstention from buying ultimately determines what should be produced and in what quantity and quality. Those shops and plants which cater exclusively or predominantly to the wealthier citizens' demand for refined luxuries play merely a subordinate role in the economic setting of the market economy. They never attain the size of big business. Big business always serves—directly or indirectly—the masses.

It is this ascension of the multitude in which the radical social change brought about by the "Industrial Revolution" consists.

Those underlings who in all the preceding ages of history had formed the herds of slaves and serfs, of paupers and beggars, became the buying public, for whose favor the businessmen canvass. They are the customers who are "always right," the patrons who have the power to make poor suppliers rich and rich suppliers poor.

There are in the fabric of a market economy not sabotaged by the nostrums of governments and politicians no grandees and squires keeping the populace in submission, collecting tributes and imposts, and gaudily feasting while the villains must put up with the crumbs. The profit system makes those men prosper who have succeeded in filling the wants of the people in the best possible and cheapest way. Wealth can be acquired only by serving the consumers. The capitalists lose their funds as soon as they fail to invest them in those lines in which they satisfy best the demands of the public. In a daily repeated plebiscite in which every penny gives a right to vote the consumers determine who should own and run the plants, shops and farms. The control of the material means of production is a social function, subject to the confirmation or revocation by the sovereign consumers.

This is what the modern concept of freedom means. Every adult is free to fashion his life according to his own plans. He is not forced to live according to the plan of a planning authority enforcing its unique plan by the police, i.e., the social apparatus of compulsion and coercion. What restricts the individual's freedom is not other people's violence or threat of violence, but the physiological structure of his body and the inescapable nature-given scarcity of the factors of production. It is obvious that man's discretion to shape his fate can never trespass the limits drawn by what are called the laws of nature.

To establish these facts does not amount to a justification of the individual freedom from the point of view of any absolute standards or metaphysical notions. It does not express any judgment on the fashionable doctrines of the advocates of totalitarianism, whether "right" or "left." It does not deal with their assertion that the masses are too stupid and ignorant to know what would serve best their "true" needs and interests and badly need a guardian, the government, lest they hurt themselves. Neither does it enter into a scrutiny of the statements that there are supermen available for the office of such guardianship.

2. The Urge for Economic Betterment

Under capitalism the common man enjoys amenities which in ages gone by were unknown and therefore inaccessible even to the richest people. But, of course, these motorcars, television sets and refrigerators do not make a man happy. In the instant in which he acquires them, he may feel happier than he did before. But as soon as some of his wishes are satisfied, new wishes spring up. Such is human nature.

Few Americans are fully aware of the fact that their country enjoys the highest standard of living and that the way of life of the average American appears as fabulous and out of the reach to the immense majority of people inhabiting non-capitalistic countries. Most people belittle what they have and could possibly acquire, and crave those things which are inaccessible to them. It would be idle to lament this insatiable appetite for more and more goods. This lust is precisely the impulse which leads man on the way toward economic betterment. To content oneself with what one has already got or can easily get, and to abstain apathetically from any attempts to improve one's own material conditions, is not a virtue. Such an attitude is rather animal behavior than conduct of reasonable human beings. Man's most characteristic mark is that he never ceases in endeavors to advance his well-being by purposive activity.

However, these endeavors must be fitted for the purpose. They must be suitable to bring about the effects aimed at. What is wrong with most of our contemporaries is not that they are passionately longing for a richer supply of various goods, but that they choose inappropriate means for the attainment of this end. They are misled by spurious ideologies. They favor policies which are contrary to their own *rightly understood* vital interests. Too dull to see the inevitable *long-run* consequences of their conduct, they find delight in its passing short-run effects. They advocate measures which are bound to result finally in general impoverishment, in the disintegration of social cooperation under the principle of the division of labor and in a return to barbarism.

There is but one means available to improve the material conditions of mankind: to accelerate the growth of capital accumulated as against the growth in population. The greater the amount of capital invested per head of the worker, the more and the better goods can be produced and consumed. This is what capitalism, the much abused profit system, has brought about and brings about daily anew. Yet, most present-day governments and political parties are eager to destroy this system.

Why do they all loathe capitalism? Why do they, while enjoying the well-being capitalism bestows upon them, cast longing glances upon the "good old days" of the past and the miserable conditions of the present-day Russian worker?

3. Status Society and Capitalism

Before answering this question it is necessary to put into better relief the distinctive feature of capitalism as against that of a status society.

It is quite customary to liken the entrepreneurs and capitalists of the market economy to the aristocrats of a status society. The basis of the comparison is the relative riches of both groups as against the relatively straitened conditions of the rest of their fellow men. However, in resorting to this metaphor, one fails to realize the fundamental difference between aristocratic riches and "bourgeois" or capitalistic riches.

The wealth of an aristocrat is not a market phenomenon; it does not originate from supplying the consumers and cannot be withdrawn or even affected by any action on the part of the public. It stems from conquest or from largess on the part of a conqueror. It may come to an end through revocation on the part of the donor or through violent eviction on the part of another conqueror, or it may be dissipated by extravagance. The feudal lord does not serve consumers and is immune to the displeasure of the populace.

The entrepreneurs and capitalists owe their wealth to the people who patronize their businesses. They lose it inevitably as soon as other men supplant them in serving the consumers better or cheaper.

It is not the task of this essay to describe the historical conditions which brought about the institutions of caste and status, of the subdivision of peoples into hereditary groups with different ranks, rights, claims, and legally sanctified privileges or disabilities. What alone is of importance for us is the fact that the preservation of these feudal institutions was incompatible with the system of capitalism. Their abolition and the establishment of the principle of equality under the law removed the barriers that prevented mankind from enjoying all those benefits which the system of private ownership of the means of production and private enterprise makes possible.

In a society based on rank, status or caste, an individual's station in life is fixed. He is born into a certain station, and his position in society is rigidly determined by the laws and customs which assign to each member of his rank definite privileges and duties or definite disabilities. Exceptionally good or bad luck may in some rare cases elevate an individual into a higher rank or debase him into a lower rank. But as a rule, the conditions of the individual members of a definite order or rank can improve or deteriorate only with a change in the conditions of the whole membership. The individual is primarily not a Citizen of a nation; he is a member of an estate

(*Stand, état)* and only as such indirectly integrated into the body of his nation. In coming into contact with a countryman belonging to another rank, he does not feel any community. He perceives only the gulf that separates him from the other man's status. This diversity was reflected in linguistic as well as in sartorial usages. Under the *ancien régime* the European aristocrats spoke preferably French. The third estate used the vernacular, while the lower ranks of the urban population and the peasants clung to local dialects, jargons and argots which often were incomprehensible to the educated. The various ranks dressed differently. No one could fail to recognize the rank of a stranger whom he happened to see somewhere.

The main criticism leveled against the principle of equality under the law by the eulogists of the good old days is that it has abolished the privileges of rank and dignity. It has, they say, "atomized" society, dissolved its "organic" subdivisions into "amorphous" masses. The "much too many" are now supreme, and their mean materialism has superseded the noble standards of ages gone by. Money is king. Quite worthless people enjoy riches and abundance, while meritorious and worthy people go empty-handed.

This criticism tacitly implies that under the *ancien régime* the aristocrats were distinguished by their virtue and that they owed their rank and their revenues to their moral and cultural superiority. It is hardly necessary to debunk this fable. Without expressing any judgment of value, the historian cannot help emphasizing that the high aristocracy of the main European countries were the descendants of those soldiers, courtiers and courtesans who, in the religious and constitutional struggles of the sixteenth and seventeenth centuries, had cleverly sided with the party that remained victorious in their respective countries.

While the conservative and the "progressive" foes of capitalism disagree with regard to the evaluation of the old standards, they fully agree in condemning the standards of capitalistic society. As they see it, not those who deserve well of their fellow men acquire wealth and prestige, but frivolous unworthy people. Both groups pretend to aim at the substitution of fairer methods of "distribution" for the manifestly unfair methods prevailing under laissez-faire capitalism.

Now, nobody ever contended that under unhampered capitalism those fare best who, from the point of view of eternal standards of value, ought to be preferred. What the capitalistic democracy of the market brings about is not rewarding people according to their "true" merits, inherent worth and moral eminence. What makes a man more or less prosperous is not the evaluation of his contribution from any "absolute" principle of justice, but evaluation on the part of his fellow men who exclusively apply the yardstick of their own personal wants, desires and ends. It is precisely this that the democratic system of the market means. The consumers are supreme—i.e., sovereign. They want to be satisfied.

Millions of people like to drink Pinkapinka, a beverage prepared by the world-embracing Pinkapinka Company. Millions like detective stories, mystery pictures, tabloid newspapers, bull fights, boxing, whiskey, cigarettes, chewing gum. Millions vote for governments eager to arm and to wage war. Thus, the entrepreneurs who provide in the best and cheapest way all the things required for the satisfaction of these wants succeed in getting rich. What counts in the frame of the market economy is not academic judgments of value, but the valuations actually manifested by people in buying or not buying.

To the grumbler who complains about the unfairness of the market system only one piece of advice can be given: If you want to acquire wealth, then try to satisfy the public by offering them something that is cheaper or which they like better. Try to supersede Pinkapinka by mixing another beverage. Equality under the law gives you the power to challenge every millionaire. It is—in a market not sabotaged by government-imposed restrictions—exclusively your fault if you do not outstrip the chocolate king, the movie star and the boxing champion.

But if you prefer to the riches you may perhaps acquire in engaging in the garment trade or in professional boxing the satisfaction you may derive from writing poetry or philosophy, you are free to do so. Then, of course, you will not make as much money as those who serve the majority. For such is the law of the economic democracy of the market. Those who satisfy the wants of a smaller number of people only collect fewer votes—dollars—than those who satisfy the wants of more people. In money-making the movie star outstrips the philosopher; the manufacturers of Pinkapinka outstrip the composer of symphonies.

It is important to realize that the opportunity to compete for the prizes society has to dispense is a social institution. It cannot remove or alleviate the innate handicaps with which nature has discriminated against many people. It cannot change the fact that many are born sick or become disabled in later life. The biological equipment of a man rigidly restricts the field in which he can serve. The class of those who have the ability to think their own thoughts is through an unbridgeable gulf separated from the class of those who cannot.

4. *The Resentment of Frustrated Ambition*

Now we can try to understand why people loathe capitalism.

In a society based on caste and status, the individual can ascribe adverse fate to conditions beyond his own control. He is a slave because the superhuman powers that determine all becoming had assigned him this rank. It is not his doing, and there is no reason for him to be ashamed of his humbleness. His wife cannot find fault with his station. If she were to tell him: "Why are you not a duke? If you were a duke, I would be a duchess," he would reply: "If I had been born the son of a duke, I would not have married you, a slave girl, but the daughter of another duke; that you are not a duchess is exclusively your own fault; why were you not more clever in the choice of your parents?"

It is quite another thing under capitalism. Here everybody's station in life depends on his own doing. Everybody whose ambitions have not been fully gratified knows very well that he has missed chances, that he has been tried and found wanting by his fellow man. If his wife upbraids him: "Why do you make only eighty dollars a week? If you were as smart as your former pal, Paul, you would be a foreman and I would enjoy a better life," he becomes conscious of his own inferiority and feels humiliated.

The much talked about sternness of capitalism consists in the fact that it handles everybody according to his contribution to the well-being of his fellow men. The sway of the principle, *to each according to his accomplishments,* does not allow of any excuse for personal shortcomings. Everybody knows very well that there are people like himself who succeeded where he himself failed. Everybody knows that many of those whom he envies are self-made men who started from the same point from which he himself started. And, much worse, he knows that all other people know it too. He reads in the eyes of his wife and his children the silent reproach: "Why have you not been smarter?" He sees how people admire those who have been more successful than he and look with contempt or with pity on his failure.

What makes many feel unhappy under capitalism is the fact that capitalism grants to each the opportunity to attain the most desirable positions which, of course, can only be attained by a few. Whatever a man may have gained for himself, it is mostly a mere fraction of what his ambition has impelled him to win. There are always before his eyes people who have succeeded where he failed. There are fellows who have outstripped him and against whom he nurtures, in his subconsciousness, inferiority complexes. Such is the attitude of the tramp against the man with a regular job, the factory hand against the foreman, the executive against the vice-president, the vice-president against the company's president, the man who is worth three hundred thousand dollars against the millionaire and so on. Everybody's self-reliance and moral equilibrium are undermined by the spectacle of those who have given proof of greater abilities and capacities. Everybody is aware of his own defeat and insufficiency.

The long line of German authors who radically rejected the "Western" ideas of the Enlightenment and the social philosophy of rationalism, utilitarianism and laissez faire as well as the policies advanced by these schools of thought was opened by Justus Möser. One of the novel principles which aroused Möser's anger was the demand that the promotion of army officers and civil servants should depend on personal merit and ability and not on the incumbent's ancestry and noble lineage, his age and length of Service. Life in a society in which success would exclusively depend on personal merit would, says Möser, simply be unbearable. As human nature is, everybody is prone to overrate his own worth and deserts. If a man's station in life is conditioned by factors other than his inherent excellence, those who remain at the bottom of the ladder can acquiesce in this outcome and, knowing their own worth, still preserve their dignity and self-respect. But it is different if merit alone decides. Then the unsuccessful feel themselves insulted and humiliated. Hate and enmity against all those who superseded them must result.[1]

The price and market system of capitalism is such a society in which merit and achievements determine a man's success or failure. Whatever one may think of Möser's bias against the merit principle, one must admit that he was right in describing one of its psychological consequences. He had an insight into the feelings of those who had been tried and found wanting.

[1] Möser, *No Promotion According to Merit,* first published 1772. (Justus Möser's *Sämmtliche Werke,* ed. B. R. Abeken, Berlin, 1842, Vol. II, pp. 187–191.)

In order to console himself and to restore his self-assertion, such a man is in search of a scapegoat. He tries to persuade himself that he failed through no fault of his own. He is at least as brilliant, efficient and industrious as those who outshine him. Unfortunately this nefarious social order of ours does not accord the prizes to the most meritorious men; it crowns the dishonest unscrupulous scoundrel, the swindler, the exploiter, the "rugged individualist." What made himself fail was his honesty. He was too decent to resort to the base tricks to which his successful rivals owe their ascendancy. As conditions are under capitalism, a man is forced to choose between virtue and poverty on the one hand, and vice and riches on the other. He, himself, thank God, chose the former alternative and rejected the latter.

This search for a scapegoat is an attitude of people living under the social order which treats everybody according to his contribution to the well-being of his fellow men and where thus everybody is the founder of his own fortune. In such a society each member whose ambitions have not been fully satisfied resents the fortune of all those who succeeded better. The fool releases these feelings in slander and defamation. The more sophisticated do not indulge in personal calumny. They sublimate their hatred into a philosophy, the philosophy of anti-capitalism, in order to render inaudible the inner voice that tells them that their failure is entirely their own fault. Their fanaticism in defending their critique of capitalism is precisely due to the fact that they are fighting their own awareness of its falsity.

The suffering from frustrated ambition is peculiar to people living in a society of equality under the law. It is not caused by equality under the law, but by the fact that in a society of equality under the law the inequality of men with regard to intellectual abilities, will power and application becomes visible. The gulf between what a man is and achieves and what he thinks of his own abilities and achievements is pitilessly revealed. Daydreams of a "fair" world which would treat him according to his "real worth" are the refuge of all those plagued by a lack of self-knowledge.

5. *The Resentment of the Intellectuals*

The common man as a rule does not have the opportunity of consorting with people who have succeeded better than he has. He moves in the circle of other common men. He never meets his boss socially. He never learns from personal experience how different an entrepreneur or an executive is with regard to all those abilities and faculties which are required for successfully serving the consumers. His envy and the resentment it engenders are not directed against a living being of flesh and blood, but against pale abstractions like "management," "capital" and "Wall Street." It is impossible to abominate such a faint shadow with the same bitterness of feeling that one may bear against a fellow creature whom one encounters daily.

It is different with people whom special conditions of their occupation or their family affiliation bring into personal contact with the winners of the prizes which—as they believe—by rights should have been given to themselves. With them the feelings of frustrated ambition become especially poignant because they engender hatred of concrete living beings. They loathe capitalism because it has assigned to this other man the position they themselves would like to have.

Such is the case with those people who are commonly called the intellectuals. Take for instance the physicians. Daily routine and experience make every doctor cognizant of the fact that there exists a hierarchy in which all medical men are graded according to their merits and achievements. Those more eminent than he himself is, those whose methods and innovations he must learn and practice in order to be up to date were his classmates in the medical school, they served with him as internes, they attend with him the meetings of medical associations. He meets them at the bedside of patients as well as in social gatherings. Some of them are his personal friends or related to him, and they all behave toward him with the utmost civility and address him as their dear colleague. But they tower far above him in the appreciation of the public and often also in height of income. They have outstripped him and now belong to another class of men. When he compares himself with them, he feels humiliated. But he must watch himself carefully lest anybody notice his resentment and envy. Even the slightest indication of such feelings would be looked upon as very bad manners and would depreciate him in the eyes of everybody. He must swallow down his mortification and divert his wrath toward a vicarious target. He indicts society's economic organization, the nefarious system of capitalism. But for this unfair regime his abilities and talents, his zeal and his achievements would have brought him the rich reward they deserve.

It is the same with many lawyers and teachers, artists and actors, writers and journalists, architects and scientific research workers, engineers and chemists. They, too, feel frustrated because they are vexed by the ascendancy of their more successful colleagues, their former schoolfellows and cronies. Their resentment is deepened by precisely those codes of professional conduct and ethics that throw a veil of comradeship and colleagueship over the reality of competition.

To understand the intellectual's abhorrence of capitalism one must realize that in his mind this system is incarnated in a definite number of compeers whose success he resents and whom he makes responsible for the frustration of his own farflung ambitions. His passionate dislike of capitalism is a mere blind for his hatred of some successful "colleagues."

6. *The Anti-capitalistic Bias of American Intellectuals*

The anticapitalistic bias of the intellectuals is a phenomenon not limited to one or a few countries only. But it is more general and more bitter in the United States than it is in the European countries. To explain this rather surprising fact one must deal with what one calls "society" or, in French, also *le monde.*

In Europe "society" includes all those eminent in any sphere of activity. Statesmen and parliamentary leaders, the heads of the various departments of the civil service, publishers and editors of the main newspapers and magazines, prominent writers, scientists, artists, actors, musicians, engineers, lawyers and physicians form together with outstanding businessmen and scions of aristocratic and patrician families what is considered the good society. They come into contact with one another at dinner and tea parties, charity balls and bazaars, at first-nights, and varnishing- days; they frequent the same restaurants, hotels and resorts. When they meet, they take their pleasure in conversation about intellectual matters, a mode of social intercourse first developed in Italy of the Renaissance, perfected in the Parisian salons and later imitated by the "society" of all important cities of Western and Central Europe. New ideas and ideologies find their response in these social gatherings before they begin to influence broader circles. One cannot deal with the history of the fine arts and literature in the nineteenth century without analyzing the role "society" played in encouraging or discouraging their protagonists.

Access to European society is open to everybody who has distinguished himself in any field. It may be easier to people of noble ancestry and great wealth than to commoners with modest incomes. But neither riches nor titles can give to a member of this set the rank and prestige that is the reward of great personal distinction. The stars of the Parisian salons are not the millionaires, but the members of the Académie Française. The intellectuals prevail and the others feign at least a lively interest in intellectual concerns.

Society in this sense is foreign to the American scene. What is called "society" in the United States almost exclusively consists of the richest families. There is little social intercourse between the successful businessmen and the nation's eminent authors, artists and scientists. Those listed in the Social Register do not meet socially the molders of public opinion and the harbingers of the ideas that will determine the future of the nation. Most of the "socialites" are not interested in books and ideas. When they meet and do not play cards, they gossip about persons and talk more about sports than about cultural matters. But even those who are not averse to reading, consider writers, scientists and artists as people with whom they do not want to consort. An almost unsurmountable gulf separates "society" from the intellectuals.

It is possible to explain the emergence of this situation historically. But such an explanation does not alter the facts. Neither can it remove or alleviate the resentment with which the intellectuals react to the contempt in which they are held by the members of "society." American authors or scientists are prone to consider the wealthy businessman as a barbarian, as a man exclusively intent upon making money. The professor despises the alumni who are more interested in the university's football team than in its scholastic achievements. He feels insulted if he learns that the coach gets a higher salary than an eminent professor of philosophy. The men whose research has given rise to new methods of production hate the businessmen who are merely interested in the cash value of their research work. It is very significant that such a large number of American research physicists sympathize with socialism or communism. As they are ignorant of economics and realize that the university teachers of economics are also opposed to what they disparagingly call the profit system, no other attitude can be expected from them.

If a group of people secludes itself from the rest of the nation, especially also from its intellectual leaders, in the way American "socialites" do, they unavoidably become the target of rather hostile criticisms on the part of those whom they keep out of their own circles. The exclusivism practiced by the American rich has made them in a certain sense outcasts. They may take a vain pride in their own distinction. What they fail to see is that their self-chosen segregation isolates them and kindles animosities which make the intellectuals inclined to favor anticapitalistic policies.

7. The Resentment of the White-Collar Workers

Besides being harassed by the general hatred of capitalism common to most people, the white-collar worker labors under two special afflictions peculiar to his own category.

Sitting behind a desk and committing words and figures to paper, he is prone to overrate the significance of his work. Like the boss he writes and reads what other fellows have put on paper and talks directly or over the telephone with other people. Full of conceit, he imagines himself to belong to the enterprise's managing elite and compares his own tasks with those of his boss. As a "worker by brain" he looks arrogantly down upon the manual worker whose hands are calloused and soiled. It makes him furious to notice that many of these manual laborers get higher pay and are more respected than he himself. What a shame, he thinks, that capitalism does not appraise his "intellectual" work according to its "true" value and fondles the simple drudgery of the "uneducated".

In nursing such atavistic ideas about the significance of office work and manual work, the white-collar man shuts his eyes to a realistic evaluation of the situation. He does not see that his own clerical job consists in the performance of routine tasks which require but a simple training, while the "hands" whom he envies are the highly skilled mechanics and technicians who know how to handle the intricate machines and contrivances of modern industry. It is precisely this complete misconstruction of the real State of affairs that discloses the clerk's lack of insight and power of reasoning.

On the other hand, the clerical worker, like professional people, is plagued by daily contact with men who have succeeded better than he. He sees some of his fellow employees who started from the same level with him make a career within the hierarchy of the office while he remains at the bottom. Only yesterday Paul was in the same rank with him. Today Paul has a more important and better paid assignment. And yet, he thinks, Paul is in every regard inferior to himself. Certainly, he concludes, Paul owes his advancement to those mean tricks and artifices that can further a man's career only under this unfair system of capitalism which all books and newspapers, all scholars and politicians denounce as the root of all mischief and misery.

The classical expression of the clerks' conceit and their fanciful belief that their own subaltern jobs are a part of the entrepreneurial activities and congeneric with the work of their bosses is to be found in Lenin's description of the "control of production and distribution" as provided by his most popular essay. Lenin himself and most of his fellow-conspirators never learned anything about the operation of the market economy and never wanted to. All they knew about capitalism was that Marx had described it as the worst of all evils. They were professional revolutionaries. The only sources of their earnings were the party funds which were fed by voluntary and more often involuntary—extorted—contributions and subscriptions and by violent "expropriations." But, before 1917, as exiles in Western and Central Europe, some of the comrades occasionally held subaltern routine jobs in business firms. It was their experience—the experience of clerks who had to fill out forms and blanks, to copy letters, to enter figures into books and to file papers—which provided Lenin with all the information he had acquired about entrepreneurial activities.

Lenin correctly distinguishes between the work of the entrepreneurs on the one hand, and that of "the scientifically educated staff of engineers, agronomists and so on" on the other hand. These experts and technologists are mainly executors of orders. They obey under capitalism the capitalists, they will obey under socialism "the armed workers." The function of the capitalists and entrepreneurs is different; it is, according to Lenin, "control of production and distribution, of labor and products." Now the tasks of the entrepreneurs and capitalists are in fact the determination of the purposes for which the factors of production are to be employed in order to serve in the best possible way the wants of the consumers—i.e., to determine what should be produced, in what quantities and in what quality. However, this is not the meaning that Lenin attaches to the term "control." As a Marxian he was unaware of the problems the conduct of production activities has to face under any imaginable system of social organization: the inevitable scarcity of the factors of production, the uncertainty of future conditions for which production has to provide, and the necessity of picking out from the bewildering multitude of technological methods suitable for the attainment of ends already chosen those which obstruct as little as possible the attainment of other ends—i.e., those with which the cost of production is lowest. No allusion to these matters can be found in the writings of Marx and Engels. All that Lenin learned about business from the tales of his comrades who occasionally sat in business offices was that it required a lot of scribbling, recording and ciphering. Thus, he declares that "accounting and control" are the chief things necessary for the organizing and correct functioning of society. But "accounting and control," he goes on saying, have already been "*simplified* by capitalism to the utmost, till they have become the extraordinarily simple operations of watching, recording and issuing receipts, within the reach of anybody who can read and write and knows the first four rules of arithmetic."[2]

Here we have the philosophy of the filing clerk in its full glory.

8. *The Resentment of the "Cousins"*

On the market not hampered by the interference of external forces, the process which tends to convey control of the factors of production into the hands of the most efficient people never stops. As soon as a man or a firm begins to slacken in endeavors to meet, in the best possible way, the most urgent of the not yet properly satisfied needs of the consumers, dissipation of the wealth accumulated by previous success in such endeavors sets in. Often this dispersion of the fortune starts already in the lifetime of the business- man when his buoyancy, energy and resourcefulness become weakened by the impact of old age, fatigue, and sickness, and his ability to adjust the conduct of his affairs to the unceasingly changing structure of the market fades away. More frequently it is the sluggishness of his heirs that fritters away the heritage. If the dull and stolid progeny do not sink back into insignificance and in spite of their incompetence remain moneyed people, they owe their prosperity to institutions and political measures which were dictated by anticapitalistic tendencies. They withdraw from the market where there is no means of preserving acquired wealth other than acquiring it anew each day in tough competition with everybody, with the already existing firms as well as with newcomers "operating on a shoestring." In buying government bonds they flee under the wings of the government which promises to safeguard them against the dangers of the market in which losses are the penalty of inefficiency.[3]

2 Cf. Lenin, *State and Revolution* (Little Lenin Library, No. 14, published by International Publishers, New York), pp. 83-84.

3 In Europe there was, until a short time ago, still another opportunity offered to make a fortune safe against clumsiness and extravagance on the part of the owner. Wealth acquired in the

However, there are families in which the eminent capacities required for entrepreneurial success are propagated through several generations. One or two of the sons or grandsons or even great-grandsons equal or excel their forebear. The ancestor's wealth is not dissipated, but grows more and more.

These cases are, of course, not frequent. They attract attention not only on account of their rarity, but also on account of the fact that men who know how to enlarge an inherited business enjoy a double prestige, the esteem shown to their fathers and that shown to themselves. Such "patricians," as they are sometimes called by people who ignore the difference between a status society and the capitalistic society, for the most part combine in their persons breeding, fineness of taste and gracious manners with the skill and industriousness of a hard-working businessman. And some of them belong to the country's or even the world's richest entrepreneurs.

It is the conditions of these few richest among these so-called patrician families which we must scrutinize in order to explain a phenomenon that plays an important role in modern anticapitalistic propaganda and machinations.

Even in these lucky families, the qualities required for the successful conduct of big business are not inherited by all sons and grandsons. As a rule only one, or at best two, of each generation are endowed with them. Then it is essential for the survival of the family's wealth and business that the conduct of affairs be entrusted to this one or to these two and that the other members be relegated to the position of mere recipients of a quota of the proceeds. The methods chosen for such arrangements vary from country to country, according to the special provisions of the national and local laws. Their effect, however, is always the same. They divide

market could be invested in big landed estates which tariffs and other legal provisions protected against competition of outsiders. Entails in Great Britain and similar settlements of succession as practiced on the Continent prevented the owner from disposing of his property to the prejudice of his heirs.

the family into two categories—those who direct the conduct of affairs and those who do not.

The second category consists as a rule of people closely related to those of the first category whom we propose to call the *bosses.* They are brothers, cousins, nephews of the bosses, more often their sisters, widowed sisters-in-law, female cousins, nieces and so on. We propose to call the members of this second category the *cousins.*

The cousins derive their revenues from the firm or corporation. But they are foreign to business life and know nothing about the problems an entrepreneur has to face. They have been brought up in fashionable boarding schools and colleges, whose atmosphere was filled by a haughty contempt for banausic money-making. Some of them pass their time in night clubs and other places of amusement, bet and gamble, feast and revel, and indulge in expensive debauchery. Others amateurishly busy themselves with painting, writing, or other arts. Thus, most of them are idle and useless people.

It is true that there have been and are exceptions, and that the achievements of these exceptional members of the group of cousins by far outweigh the scandals raised by the provoking behavior of the playboys and spendthrifts. Many of the most eminent authors, scholars and statesmen were such "gentlemen of no occupation." Free from the necessity of earning a livelihood by a gainful occupation and independent of the favor of those addicted to bigotry, they became pioneers of new ideas. Others, themselves lacking the inspiration, became the Maecenas of artists who, without the financial aid and the applause received, would not have been in a position to accomplish their creative work. The role that moneyed men played in Great Britain's intellectual and political evolution has been stressed by many historians. The milieu in which the authors and artists of nineteenth-century France lived and found encouragement was *le monde,* "society."

However, we deal here neither with the sins of the play- boys nor with the excellence of other groups of wealthy people. Our theme is the part which a special group of cousins took in the dissemination of doctrines aiming at the destruction of the market economy.

Many cousins believe that they have been wronged by the arrangements regulating their financial relation to the bosses and the family's firm. Whether these arrangements were made by the will of their father or grandfather, or by an agreement which they themselves have signed, they think that they are receiving too little and the bosses too much. Unfamiliar with the nature of business and the market, they are—with Marx—convinced that capital automatically "begets profits." They do not see any reason why those members of the family who are in charge of the conduct of affairs should earn more than they. Too dull to appraise correctly the meaning of balance sheets and profit and loss accounts, they suspect in every act of the bosses a sinister attempt to cheat them and to deprive them of their birthright. They quarrel with them continually.

It is not astonishing that the bosses lose their temper. They are proud of their success in overcoming all the obstacles which governments and labor unions place in the way of big business. They are fully aware of the fact that, but for their efficiency and zeal, the firm would either have long since gone astray or the family would have been forced to sell out. They believe that the cousins should do justice to their merits, and they find their complaints simply impudent and outrageous.

The family feud between the bosses and the cousins concerns only the members of the clan. But it attains general importance when the cousins, in order to annoy the bosses, join the anticapitalistic camp and provide the funds for all kinds of "progressive" ventures. The cousins are enthusiastic in supporting strikes, even strikes in the factories from which their own revenues originate.[4] It is a well-known fact that most of the "progressive" magazines and many

4 "Limousines with liveried chauffeurs delivered earnest ladies to the picket lines, sometimes *in strikes against businesses which helped to pay for the limousines.*" Eugene Lyons, *The Red Decade*, New York, 1941, p. 186. (Italics mine.)

"progressive" newspapers entirely depend on the subsidies lavishly granted by them. These cousins endow progressive universities and colleges and institutes for "social research" and sponsor all sorts of communist party activities. As "parlor socialists" and "penthouse Bolsheviks," they play an important role in the "proletarian army" fighting against the "dismal system of capitalism."

9. *The Communism of Broadway and Hollywood*

The many to whom capitalism gave a comfortable income and leisure are yearning for entertainment. Crowds throng to the theatres. There is money in show business. Popular actors and playwrights enjoy a six-figure income. They live in palatial houses with butlers and swimming pools. They certainly are not "prisoners of starvation." Yet Hollywood and Broadway, the world-famous centers of the entertainment industry, are hotbeds of communism. Authors and performers are to be found among the most bigoted supporters of Sovietism.

Various attempts have been made to explain this phenomenon. There is in most of these interpretations a grain of truth. However, they all fail to take account of the main motive that drives champions of the stage and the screen into the ranks of revolutionaries.

Under capitalism, material success depends on the appreciation of a man's achievements on the part of the sovereign consumers. In this regard there is no difference between the services rendered by a manufacturer and those rendered by a producer, an actor or a playwright. Yet the awareness of this dependence makes those in the show business much more uneasy than those supplying the customers with tangible amenities. The manufacturers of tangible goods know that their products are purchased because of certain physical properties. They may reasonably expect that the public will continue to ask for these commodities as long as nothing better or cheaper is offered to them, for it is unlikely that the needs which these goods satisfy will change in the near future. The State of the market for these goods can, to some extent, be anticipated by intelligent entrepreneurs. They can, with a degree of confidence, look into the future.

It is another thing with entertainment. People long for amusement because they are bored. And nothing makes them so weary as amusements with which they are already familiar. The essence of the entertainment industry is variety. The patrons applaud most what is new and therefore unexpected and surprising. They are capricious and unaccountable. They disdain what they cherished yesterday. A tycoon of the stage or the screen must always fear the waywardness of the public. He awakes rich and famous one morning and may be forgotten the next day. He knows very well that he depends entirely on the whims and fancies of a crowd hankering after merriment. He is always agitated by anxiety. Like the master-builder in Ibsen's play, he fears the unknown newcomers, the vigorous youths who will supplant him in the favor of the public.

It is obvious that there is no relief from what makes these stage people uneasy. Thus they catch at a straw. Communism, some of them think, will bring their deliverance. Is it not a system that makes all people happy? Do not very eminent men declare that all the evils of mankind are caused by capitalism and will be wiped out by communism? Are not they themselves hard-working people, comrades of all other working men?

It may be fairly assumed that none of the Hollywood and Broadway communists has ever studied the writings of any socialist author and still less any serious analysis of the market economy. But it is this very fact that, to these glamour girls, dancers and singers, to these authors and producers of comedies, moving pictures and songs, gives the strange illusion that their particular grievances will disappear as soon as the "expropriators" will be expropriated.

There are people who blame capitalism for the stupidity and crudeness of many products of the entertainment industry. There is no need to argue this point. But it is note- worthy to remember that no other American milieu was more enthusiastic in the endorsement of communism than that of people cooperating in the production of these silly plays and films. When a future historian searches for those little significant facts which Taine appreciated highly as source material, he should not neglect to mention the role which the world's most famous strip-tease artist played in the American radical movement.[5]

5 Cf. Eugene Lyons, l.c., p. 293.

II.
The Ordinary Man's Social Philosophy

1. The Capitalism as It Is and as It Is Seen by the Common Man

The emergence of economics as a new branch of knowledge was one of the most portentous events in the history of mankind. In paving the way for private capitalistic enterprise it transformed within a few generations all human affairs more radically than the preceding ten thousand years had done. From the day of their birth to the day of their demise, the denizens of a capitalistic country are every minute benefited by the marvelous achievements of the capitalistic ways of thinking and acting.

The most amazing thing concerning the unprecedented change in earthly conditions brought about by capitalism is the fact that it was accomplished by a small number of authors and a hardly greater number of statesmen who had assimilated their teachings. Not only the sluggish masses but also most of the businessmen who, by their trading, made the laissez-faire principles effective failed to comprehend the essential features of their operation. Even in the heyday of liberalism only a few people had a full grasp of the functioning of the market economy. Western civilization adopted capitalism upon recommendation on the part of a small élite.

There were, in the first decades of the nineteenth century, many people who viewed their own unfamiliarity with the problems concerned as a serious shortcoming and were anxious to redress it. In the years between Waterloo and Sebastopol, no other books were more eagerly absorbed in Great Britain than treatises on economics. But the vogue soon subsided. The subject was unpalatable to the general reader.

Economics is so different from the natural sciences and technology on the one hand, and history and jurisprudence on the other hand, that it seems strange and repulsive to the beginner. Its heuristic singularity is viewed with suspicion by those whose research work is performed in laboratories or in archives and libraries. Its epistemological singularity appears nonsensical to the narrow-minded fanatics of positivism. People would like to find in an economics book knowledge that perfectly fits into their preconceived image of what economics ought to be, viz., a discipline shaped according to the logical structure of physics or of biology. They are bewildered and desist from seriously grappling with problems the analysis of which requires an unwonted mental exertion.

The result of this ignorance is that people ascribe all improvements in economic conditions to the progress of the natural Sciences and technology. As they see it, there pre- vails in the course of human history a self-acting tendency toward progressing advancement of the experimental natural Sciences and their application to the solution of technological problems. This tendency is irresistible, it is inherent in the destiny of mankind, and its operation takes effect whatever the political and economic organization of society may be. As they see it, the unprecedented technological improvements of the last two hundred years were not caused or furthered by the economic policies of the age. They were not an achievement of classical liberalism, free trade, laissez faire and capitalism.

They will therefore go on under any other system of society's economic organization.

The doctrines of Marx received approval simply because they adopted this popular interpretation of events and clothed it with a pseudophilosophical veil that made it gratifying both to Hegelian spiritualism and to crude materialism. In the scheme of Marx the "material productive forces" are a superhuman entity independent of the will and the actions of men. They go their own way that is prescribed by the inscrutable and inevitable laws of a higher power. They change mysteriously and force mankind to adjust its social organization to these changes; for the material productive forces shun one thing: to be enchained by mankind's social organization. The essential content of history is the struggle of the material productive forces to be freed from the social bonds by which they are fettered.

Once upon a time, teaches Marx, the material productive forces were embodied in the shape of the hand mill, and then they arranged human affairs according to the pattern of feudalism. When, later, the unfathomable laws that determine the evolution of the material productive forces substituted the steam mill for the hand mill, feudalism had to give way to capitalism. Since then the material productive forces have developed further, and their present shape imperatively requires the substitution of socialism for capitalism. Those who try to check the socialist revolution are committed to a hopeless task. It is impossible to stem the tide of historical progress.

The ideas of the so-called leftist parties differ from one another in many ways. But they agree in one point. They all look upon progressing material improvement as upon a self-acting process. The American union member takes his standard of living for granted. Fate has determined that he should enjoy amenities which were denied even to the most prosperous people of earlier generations and are still denied to non-Americans. It does not occur to him that the "rugged individualism" of big business may have played some role in the emergence of what he calls the "American way of life." In his eyes "management" represents the unfair claims of the "exploiters" who are intent upon depriving him of his birthright. There is, he thinks, in the course of historical evolution an irrepressible tendency toward a continuous in- crease in the "productivity" of his labor. It is obvious that the fruits of this betterment by rights belong exclusively to him. It is his merit that—in the age of capitalism—the quotient of the value of the products turned out by the Processing industries divided by the number of hands employed tended toward an increase.

The truth is that the increase in what is called the productivity of labor is due to the employment of better tools and machines. A hundred workers in a modern factory produce per unit of time a multiple of what a hundred workers used to produce in the workshops of precapitalistic craftsmen. This improvement is not conditioned by higher skill, competence or application on the part of the individual worker. (It is a fact that the proficiency needed by medieval artisans towered far above that of many categories of present-day factory hands.) It is due to the employment of more efficient tools and machines which, in turn, is the effect of the accumulation and investment of more capital.

The terms capitalism, capital, and capitalists were employed by Marx and are today employed by most people—also by the official propaganda agencies of the United States government—with an opprobrious connotation. Yet these words pertinently point toward the main factor whose operation produced all the marvelous achievements of the last two hundred years: the unprecedented improvement of the average standard of living for a continually increasing population. What distinguishes modern industrial conditions in the capitalistic countries from those of the precapitalistic ages as well as from those prevailing today in the so-called under-developed countries is the amount of the supply of capital. No technological improvement can be put to work if the capital required has not previously been accumulated by saving.

Saving, capital accumulation, is the agency that has transformed step by step the awkward search for food on the part of savage cave dwellers into the modern ways of industry. The pacemakers of this evolution were the ideas that created the institutional framework within which capital accumulation was rendered safe by the principle of private ownership of the means of production. Every step forward on the way toward prosperity is the effect of saving. The most ingenious technological inventions would be practically useless if the capital goods required for their utilization had not been accumulated by saving.

The entrepreneurs employ the capital goods made available by the savers for the most economical satisfaction of the most urgent among the not yet satisfied wants of the consumers. Together with the technologists, intent upon perfecting the methods of processing, they play, next to the savers themselves, an active part in the course of events that is called economic progress. The rest of mankind profit from the activities of these three classes of pioneers. But whatever their own doings may be, they are only beneficiaries of changes to the emergence of which they did not contribute anything.

The characteristic feature of the market economy is the fact that it allots the greater part of the improvements brought about by the endeavors of the three progressive classes—those saving, those investing the capital goods and those elaborating new methods for the employment of capital goods—to the nonprogressive majority of people. Capital accumulation exceeding the increase in population raises, on the one hand, the marginal productivity of labor and, on the other hand, cheapens the products. The market process provides the common man with the opportunity to enjoy the fruits of other peoples' achievements. It forces the three progressive classes to serve the nonprogressive majority in the best possible way.

Everybody is free to join the ranks of the three progressive classes of a capitalist society. These classes are not closed castes. Membership in them is not a privilege conferred on the individual by a higher authority or inherited from one's ancestors. These classes are not clubs, and the ins have no power to keep out any newcomer. What is needed to become a capitalist, an entrepreneur or a deviser of new technological methods is brains and will power. The heir of a wealthy man enjoys a certain advantage as he starts under more favorable conditions than others. But his task in the rivalry of the market is not easier, but sometimes even more wearisome and less remunerative than that of a newcomer. He has to reorganize his inheritance in order to adjust it to the changes in market conditions. Thus, for instance, the problems that the heir of a railroad "empire" had to face were, in the last decades, certainly more knotty than those encountered by the man who started from scratch in trucking or in air transportation.

The popular philosophy of the common man misrepresents all these facts in the most lamentable way. As John Doe sees it, all those new industries that are supplying him with amenities unknown to his father carne into being by some mythical agency called progress. Capital accumulation, entrepreneurship and technological ingenuity did not contribute anything to the spontaneous generation of prosperity. If any man has to be credited with what John Doe considers as the rise in the productivity of labor, then it is the man on the assembly line. Unfortunately, in this sinful world there is exploitation of man by man. Business skims the cream and leaves, as the Communist Manifesto points out, to the creator of all good things, to the manual worker, not more than "he requires for his maintenance and for the propagation of his race." Consequently, "the modern worker, instead of rising with the progress of industry, sinks deeper and deeper.... He becomes a pauper, and pauperism develops more rapidly than population and wealth." The authors of this description of capitalistic industry are praised at universities as the greatest philosophers and benefactors of mankind and their teachings are accepted with reverential awe by the millions whose homes, besides other gadgets, are equipped with radio and television sets.

The worst exploitation, say professors, "labor" leaders and politicians, is effected by big business. They fail to realize that the characteristic mark of big business is mass production for the satisfaction of the needs of the masses. Under capitalism the workers themselves, directly or indirectly, are the main consumers of all those things that the factories are turning out.

In the early days of capitalism there was still a considerable time lag between the emergence of an innovation and its becoming accessible to the masses. About sixty years ago Gabriel Tarde was right in pointing out that an industrial innovation is the fancy of a minority before it becomes the need of everybody; what was considered first as an extravagance turns later into a customary requisite of all and sundry. This statement was still correct with regard to the popularization of the automobile. But big-scale production by big business has shortened and almost eliminated this time lag. Modern innovations can only be produced profitably according to the methods of mass production and hence become accessible to the many at the very moment of their practical inauguration. There was, for instance, in the United States no sensible period in which the enjoyment of such innovations as television, nylon stockings or canned baby food was reserved to a minority of the well-to-do. Big business tends, in fact, toward a standardization of the peoples' ways of consumption and enjoyment.

Nobody is needy in the market economy because of the fact that some people are rich. The riches of the rich are not the cause of the poverty of anybody. The process that makes some people rich is, on the contrary, the corollary of the process that improves many peoples' want satisfaction. The entrepreneurs, the capitalists and the technologists prosper as far as they succeed in best supplying the consumers.

2. *The Anti-capitalistic Front*

From the very beginnings of the socialist movement and the endeavors to revive the interventionist policies of the precapitalistic ages, both socialism and interventionism were utterly discredited in the eyes of those conversant with economic theory. But the ideas of the revolutionaries and reformers found approval with the immense majority of ignorant people exclusively driven by the most powerful human passions of envy and hatred.

The social philosophy of the Enlightenment that paved the way for the realization of the liberal program—economic freedom, consummated in the market economy (capitalism), and its constitutional corollary, representative government—did not suggest the annihilation of the three old powers: the monarchy, the aristocracy and the churches. The European liberais aimed at the substitution of the parliamentary monarchy for royal absolutism, not at the establishment of republican government. They wanted to abolish the privileges of the aristocrats, but not to deprive them of their titles, their escutcheons and their estates. They were eager to grant to everybody freedom of conscience and to put an end to the persecution of dissenters and heretics, but they were anxious to give to all churches and denominations perfect freedom in the pursuit of their spiritual objectives. Thus the three great powers of the *ancien régime* were preserved. One might have expected that princes, aristocrats and clergymen who indefatigably professed their conservatism would be prepared to oppose the socialist attack upon the essentials of Western civilization. After all, the harbingers of socialism did not shrink from disclosing that under socialist totalitarianism no room would be left for what they called the remnants of tyranny, privilege and superstition.

However, even with these privileged groups resentment and envy were more intense than cool reasoning. They virtually joined hands with the socialists disregarding the fact that socialism aimed also at the confiscation of their holdings and that there cannot be any religious freedom under a totalitarian system. The Hohenzollern in Germany inaugurated a policy that an American observer called monarchical socialism.[6] The autocratic Romanoffs of Russia toyed with labor unionism as a weapon to fight the "bourgeois" endeavors to establish representative government.[7] In every European country the aristocrats were virtually cooperating with the enemies of capitalism. Everywhere eminent theologians tried to discredit the free enterprise system and thus, by implication, to support either socialism or radical interventionism. Some of the outstanding leaders of present-day Protestantism—Barth and Brunner in Switzerland, Niebuhr and Tillich in the United States, and the late Archbishop of Canterbury, William Temple—openly condemn capitalism and even charge the alleged failures of capitalism with the responsibility for all the excesses of Russian Bolshevism.

One may wonder whether Sir William Harcourt was right when, more than sixty years ago, he proclaimed: We are all socialists now. But today governments, political parties, teachers and writers, militant antitheists as well as Christian theologians are almost unanimous in passionately rejecting the market economy and praising the alleged benefits of State omnipotence. The rising generation is brought up in an environment that is engrossed in socialist ideas.

The influence of the pro-socialist ideology comes to light in the way in which public opinion, almost without any exception, explains the reasons that induce people to join the socialist or communist parties. In dealing with domestic politics, one assumes that, "naturally and necessarily," those who are not rich favor the radical programs—planning, socialism, communism—while only the rich have reason to vote for the preservation of the market economy. This assumption takes for granted the fundamental socialist idea that

6 Cf. Elmer Roberts, *Monarchical Socialism in Germany*, New York, 1913.

7 Cf. Mania Gordon, *Workers Before and After Lenin*, New York, 1941, pp. 30 ff.

the economic interests of the masses are hurt by the operation of capitalism for the sole benefit of the "exploiters" and that socialism will improve the common man's standard of living.

However, people do not ask for socialism because they *know* that socialism will improve their conditions, and they do not reject capitalism because they *know* that it is a system prejudicial to their interests. They are socialists because they *believe* that socialism will improve their conditions, and they hate capitalism because they *believe* that it harms them. They are socialists because they are blinded by envy and ignorance. They stubbornly refuse to study economics and spurn the economists' devastating critique of the socialist plans because, in their eyes, economics, being an abstract theory, is simply nonsense. They pretend to trust only in experience. But they no less stubbornly refuse to take cognizance of the undeniable facts of experience, viz., that the common man's standard of living is incomparably higher in capitalistic American than in the socialist paradise of the Soviets.

In dealing with conditions in the economically backward countries people display the same faulty reasoning. They think that these peoples must "naturally" sympathize with communism because they are poverty stricken. Now it is obvious that the poor nations want to get rid of their penury. Aiming at an improvement of their unsatisfactory conditions, they ought therefore to adopt that system of society's economic organization which best warrants the attainment of this end; they ought to decide in favor of capitalism. But, deluded by spurious anticapitalistic ideas, they are favorably disposed to communism. It is paradoxical indeed that the leaders of these Oriental peoples, while casting longing glances at the prosperity of the Western nations, reject the methods that made the West prosperous and are enraptured by Russian communism that is instrumental in keeping the Russians and their satellites poor. It is still more paradoxical that Americans, enjoying the products of capitalistic big business, exalt the Soviet system and consider it quite "natural" that the poor nations of Asia and Africa should prefer communism to capitalism.

People may disagree on the question of whether everybody ought to study economics seriously. But one thing is certain. A man who publicly talks or writes about the opposition between capitalism and socialism without having fully familiarized himself with all that economics has to say about these issues is an irresponsible babbler.

III.
Literature Under Capitalism

1. *The Market for Literary Products*

Capitalism provides many with the opportunity to display initiative. While the rigidity of a status society enjoins on everybody the unvarying performance of routine and does not tolerate any deviation from traditional patterns of conduct, capitalism encourages the innovator. Profit is the prize of successful deviation from customary types of procedure; loss is the penalty of those who sluggishly cling to obsolete methods. The individual is free to show what he can do in a better way than other people.

However, this freedom of the individual is limited. It is an outcome of the democracy of the market and therefore depends on the appreciation of the individual's achievements on the part of the sovereign consumers. What pays on the market is not the good performance as such, but the performance recognized as good by a sufficient number of customers. If the buying public is too dull to appreciate duly the worth of a product, however excellent, all the trouble and expense were spent in vain.

Capitalism is essentially a system of mass production for the satisfaction of the needs of the masses. It pours a horn of plenty upon the common man. It has raised the average standard of living to a height never dreamed of in earlier ages. It has made accessible to millions of people enjoyments which a few generations ago were only within the reach of a small elite.

The outstanding example is provided by the evolution of a broad market for all kinds of literature. Literature—in the widest sense of the term—is today a commodity asked for by millions. They read newspapers, magazines and books, they listen to the broadcasts and they fill the theatres. Authors, producers and actors who gratify the public's wishes earn considerable revenues. Within the frame of the social division of labor a new subdivision evolved, the species of the literati, i.e., people making a living from writing. These authors sell their services or the product of their effort on the market just as all other specialists are selling their services or their products. They are in their very capacity as writers firmly integrated into the cooperative body of the market society.

In the precapitalistic ages writing was an unremunerative art. Blacksmiths and shoemakers could make a living, but authors could not. Writing was a liberal art, a hobby, but not a profession. It was a noble pursuit of wealthy people, of kings, grandees and statesmen, of patricians and other gentlemen of independent means. It was practiced in spare time by bishops and monks, university teachers and soldiers. The penniless man whom an irresistible impulse prompted to write had first to secure some source of revenue other than authorship. Spinoza ground lenses. The two Mills, father and son, worked in the London offices of the East India Company. But most of the poor authors lived from the openhandedness of wealthy friends of the arts and Sciences. Kings and princes vied with one another in patronizing poets and writers. The courts were the asylum of literature.

It is a historical fact that this system of patronage granted to the authors full freedom of expression. The patrons did not venture to impose upon their proteges their own philosophy and their own standards of taste and ethics. They were often eager to protect them against the church authorities. At least it was possible for an author whom one or several courts had banned to find refuge with a rival court.

Nonetheless, the vision of philosophers, historians and poets moving in the midst of courtiers and depending on the good graces of a despot is not very edifying. The old liberals hailed the evolution of a market for literary products as an essential part of the process which emancipated men from the tutelage of kings and aristocrats. Henceforth, they thought, the judgment of the educated classes will be supreme. What a wonderful prospect! A new florescence seemed to be dawning.

2. Success on the Book Market

However, there were some flaws in this picture.

Literature is not conformism, but dissent. Those authors who merely repeat what everybody approves and wants to hear are of no importance. What counts alone is the innovator, the dissenter, the harbinger of things unheard of, the man who rejects the traditional standards and aims at substituting new values and ideas for old ones. He is by necessity anti-authoritarian and anti-governmental, irreconcilably opposed to the immense majority of his contemporaries. He is precisely the author whose books the greater part of the public does not buy.

Whatever one may think about Marx and Nietzsche, nobody can deny that their posthumous success has been overwhelming. Yet they both would have died from starvation if they had not had other sources of income than their royalties. The dissenter and innovator has little to expect from the sale of his books on the regular market.

The tycoon of the book market is the author of fiction for the masses. It would be wrong to assume that these buyers always prefer bad books to good books. They lack discrimination and are, therefore, ready to absorb sometimes even good books. It is true that most of the novels and plays published today are mere trash. Nothing else can be expected when thousands of volumes are written every year. Our age could still some day be called an age of the flowering of literature if only one out of a thousand books published would prove to be equal to the great books of the past.

Many critics take pleasure in blaming capitalism for what they call the decay of literature. Perhaps they should rather inculpate their own inability to sift the chaff from the wheat. Are they keener than their predecessors were about a hundred years ago? Today, for instance, all critics are full of praise for Stendhal. But when Stendhal died in 1842, he was obscure and misunderstood.

Capitalism could render the masses so prosperous that they buy books and magazines. But it could not imbue them with the discernment of Maecenas or Can Grande della Scala. It is not the fault of capitalism that the common man does not appreciate uncommon books.

3. Remarks about the Detective Stories

The age in which the radical anticapitalistic movement acquired seemingly irresistible power brought about a new literary genre, the detective story. The same generation of Englishmen whose votes swept the Labour Party into office were enraptured by such authors as Edgar Wallace. One of the outstanding British socialist authors, G. D. H. Cole, is no less remarkable as an author of detective stories. A consistent Marxian would have to call the detective story—perhaps together with the Hollywood pictures, the comics and the "art" of strip-tease—the artistic superstructure of the epoch of labor unionism and socialization.

Many historians, sociologists and psychologists have tried to explain the popularity of this strange genre. The most profound of these investigations is that of Professor W. O. Aydelotte. Professor Aydelotte is right in asserting that the historical value of the detective stories is that they describe daydreams and thus shed light on the people who read them. He is no less right in suggesting that the reader identifies himself with the detective and in very general terms makes the detective an extension of his ego.[8]

Now this reader is the frustrated man who did not attain the position which his ambition impelled him to aim at. As we said already, he is prepared to console himself by blaming the injustice of the capitalist system. He failed because he is honest and law-abiding. His more lucky competitors succeeded on account of their improbity; they resorted to foul tricks which he, conscientious and stainless as he is, would never have thought of. If people only knew how crooked these arrogant upstarts are! Unfortunately their crimes remained hidden and they enjoy an undeserved reputation. But the day of judgment will come. He himself will unmask them and disclose their misdeeds.

The typical course of events in a detective story is this: A man whom all people consider as respectable and incapable of any shabby action has committed an abominable crime. Nobody suspects him. But the smart sleuth cannot be fooled. He knows everything about such sanctimonious hypocrites. He assembles all the evidence to convict the culprit. Thanks to him, the good cause finally triumphs.

The unmasking of the crook who passes himself off as a respectable citizen was, with a latent anti-bourgeois tendency, a topic often treated also at a higher literary level, e.g., by Ibsen in *The Pillars of Society*. The detective story debases the plot and introduces into it the cheap character of the self-righteous sleuth who takes delight in humiliating a man whom all people considered as an impeccable

8 Cf. William O. Aydelotte, *The Detective Story as a Historical Source.* (The Yale Review, 1949, Vol. XXXIX, pp. 76-95.)

citizen. The detective's motive is a subconscious hatred of successful "bourgeois." His counterpart are the inspectors of the government's police force. They are too dull and too prepossessed to solve the riddle. It is sometimes even implied that they are unwittingly biased in favor of the culprit because his social position strongly impresses them. The detective surmounts the obstacles which their sluggishness puts into his way. His triumph is a defeat of the authorities of the bourgeois state who have appointed such police officers.

This is why the detective story is popular with people who suffer from frustrated ambition. (There are, of course, also other readers of detective stories.) They dream day and night of how to wreak their vengeance upon successful competitors. They dream of the moment when their rival, "handcuffs around his wrist, is led away by the police." This satisfaction is vicariously given to them by the climax of the story in which they identify themselves with the detective, and the trapped murderer with the rival who superseded them.[9]

4. Freedom of the Press

Freedom of the press is one of the fundamental features of a nation of free citizens. It is one of the essential points in the political program of old classical liberalism. No one has ever succeeded in advancing any tenable objections against the reasoning of the two classical books: John Milton's *Areopagitica,* 1644, and John Stuart Mills' *On Liberty,* 1859. Unlicensed printing is the life blood of literature.

A free press can exist only where there is private control of the means of production. In a socialist commonwealth, where all publication facilities and printing presses are owned and operated

9 A significant fact is the circulation success of the so-called exposé magazines, the most recent addition to the American press. These magazines are exclusively devoted to the unmasking of secret vices and misdeeds on the part of successful people, especially of millionaires and of celebrities of the screen. According to *Newsweek,* of July 11, 1955, one of these magazines estimated its sales for the September 1955 issue at 3.8 million copies. It is obvious that the average common man rejoices in the exposure of the—real or alleged—sins of those who outshine him.

by the government, there cannot be any question of a free press. The government alone determines who should have the time and opportunity to write and what should be printed and published. Compared with the conditions prevailing in Soviet Russia even Tsarist Russia, retrospectively, looks like a country of a free press. When the Nazis performed their notorious book *auto-da-fé,* they exactly conformed to the designs of one of the great socialist authors, Cabet.[10]

As all nations are moving toward socialism, the freedom of authors is vanishing step by step. From day to day it becomes more difficult for a man to publish a book or an article, the content of which displeases the government or powerful pressure groups. The heretics are not yet "liquidated" as in Russia nor are their books burned by order of the Inquisition. Neither is there a return to the old system of censorship. The self-styled progressives have more efficient weapons at their disposal. Their foremost tool of oppression is boycotting authors, editors, publishers, booksellers, printers, advertisers and readers.

Everybody is free to abstain from reading books, magazines, and newspapers he dislikes and to recommend to other people to shun these books, magazines, and newspapers. But it is quite another thing when some people threaten other people with serious reprisals in case they should not stop patronizing certain publications and their publishers. In many countries publishers of newspapers and magazines are frightened by the prospect of a boycott on the part of labor unions. They avoid open discussion of the issue and tacitly yield to the dictates of the union bosses.[11]

These "labor" leaders are much more touchy than were the imperial and royal majesties of bygone ages. They can- not take a joke. Their touchiness has degraded the satire, the comedy and the

[10] Cf. Cabet, *Voyage en Icarie,* Paris, 1848, p. 127.

[11] About the boycott system established by the Catholic Church, cf. P. Blanshard, *American Freedom and Catholic Power,* Boston, 1949, pp. 194-198.

musical comedy of the legitimate theatre and has condemned the moving pictures to sterility.

In the *ancien régime* the theatres were free to produce Beaumarchais's mocking of the aristocracy and the immortal opera composed by Mozart. Under the second French empire, Offenbach's and Halévy's *Grandduchess of Gerolstein* parodied absolutism, militarism and court life. Napoleon III himself and some of the other European monarchs enjoyed the play that made them ridiculous. In the Victorian Age, the censor of the British theatres, the Lord Chamberlain, did not hinder the performance of Gilbert and Sullivan's musical comedies which made fun of all venerable institutions of the British system of government. Noble Lords filled the boxes while on the stage the Earl of Montararat sang: "The House of Peers made no pretence to intellectual eminence."

In our day it is out of the question to parody on the stage the powers that be. No disrespectful reflection on labor unions, cooperatives, government operated enterprises, budget deficits and other features of the welfare State is tolerated. The union bosses and the bureaucrats are sacrosanct. What is left to comedy are those topics that have made the operetta and the Hollywood farce abominable.

5. The Bigotry of the Literati

A superficial observer of present-day ideologies could easily fail to recognize the prevailing bigotry of the molders of public opinion and the machinations which render inaudible the voice of dissenters. There seems to be disagreement with regard to issues considered as important. Communists, socialists and interventionists and the various sects and schools of these parties are fighting each other with such zeal that attention is diverted from the fundamental dogmas with regard to which there is full accord among them. On the other hand, the few independent thinkers who have the courage to question these dogmas are virtually outlawed, and their ideas cannot reach the reading public. The tremendous machine of "progressive" propaganda and indoctrination has well succeeded in enforcing its taboos. The intolerant orthodoxy of the self-styled "unorthodox" schools dominates the scene.

This "unorthodox" dogmatism is a self-contradictory and confused mixture of various doctrines incompatible with one another. It is eclecticism at its worst, a garbled collection of surmises borrowed from fallacies and misconceptions long since exploded. It includes scraps from many socialist authors, both "utopian" and "scientific Marxian," from the German Historical School, the Fabians, the American Institutionalists, the French Syndicalists, the Technocrats. It repeats errors of Godwin, Carlyle, Ruskin, Bismarck, Sorel, Veblen and a host of less well known men.

The fundamental dogma of this creed declares that poverty is an outcome of iniquitous social institutions. The original sin that deprived mankind of the blissful life in the Garden of Eden was the establishment of private property and enterprise. Capitalism serves only the selfish interests of rugged exploiters. It dooms the masses of righteous men to progressing impoverishment and degradation. What is needed to make all people prosperous is the taming of the greedy exploiters by the great god called State. The "service" motive must be substituted for the "profit" motive. Fortunately, they say, no intrigues and no brutality on the part of the infernal "economic royalists" can quell the reform movement. The coming of an age of central planning is inevitable. Then there will be plenty and abundance for all. Those eager to accelerate this great transformation call themselves progressives precisely because they pretend that they are working for the realization of what is both desirable and in accordance with the inexorable laws of historical evolution. They disparage as reactionaries all those who are committed to the vain effort of stopping what they call progress.

From the point of view of these dogmas the progressives advocate certain policies which, as they pretend, could alleviate immediately the lot of the suffering masses. They recommend, e.g., credit expansion and increasing the amount of money in circulation, minimum wage rates to be decreed and enforced either by the government or by labor union pressure and violence, control of commodity prices and rents and other interventionist measures. But the economists have demonstrated that all such nostrums fail to bring about those results which their advocates want to attain. Their outcome is, *from the very point of view of those recommending them and resorting to their execution,* even more unsatisfactory than the previous state of affairs which they were designed to alter. Credit expansion results in the recurrence of economic crisis and periods of depression. Inflation makes the prices of all commodities and services soar. The attempts to enforce wage rates higher than those the unhampered market would have determined produce mass unemployment prolonged year after year. Price ceilings result in a drop in the supply of commodities affected. The economists have proved these theorems in an irrefutable way. No "progressive" pseudo-economist ever tried to refute them.

The essential charge brought by the progressives against capitalism is that the recurrence of crisis and depressions and mass unemployment are its inherent features. The demonstration that these phenomena are, on the contrary, the result of the interventionist attempts to regulate capitalism and to improve the conditions of the common man give the progressive ideology the finishing stroke. As the progressives are not in a position to advance any tenable objections to the teachings of the economists, they try to conceal them from the people and especially also from the intellectuals and the university students. Any mentioning of these heresies is strictly forbidden. Their authors are called names, and the students are dissuaded from reading their "crazy stuff."

As the progressive dogmatist sees things, there are two groups of men quarreling about how much of the "national income" each of them should take for themselves. The propertied class, the entrepreneurs and the capitalists, to whom they often refer as "management," is not prepared to leave to "labor"—i.e., the wage earners and employees—more than a trifle, just a little bit more than bare sustenance. Labor, as may easily be understood, annoyed by management's greed, is inclined to lend an ear to the radicals, to the communists, who want to expropriate management entirely. However, the majority of the working class is moderate enough not to indulge in excessive radicalism. They reject communism and are ready to content themselves with less than the total confiscation of "unearned" income. They aim at a middle-of-the-road solution, at planning, the welfare state, socialism. In this controversy the intellectuals who allegedly do not belong to either of the two opposite camps are called to act as arbiters. They—the professors, the representatives of science, and the writers, the representatives of literature—must shun the extremists of each group, those who recommend capitalism as well as those who endorse communism. They must side with the moderates. They must stand for planning, the welfare state, socialism, and they must support all measures designed to curb the greed of management and to prevent it from abusing its economic power.

There is no need to enter anew into a detailed analysis of all the fallacies and contradictions implied in this way of thinking. It is enough to single out three fundamental errors.

First: The great ideological conflict of our age is not a struggle about the distribution of the "national income." It is not a quarrel between two classes each of which is eager to appropriate to itself the greatest possible portion of a total sum available for distribution. It is a dissension concerning the choice of the most adequate system of society's economic organization. The question is, which of the two systems, capitalism or socialism, warrants a higher productivity of human efforts to improve people's standard of living. The question is, also, whether socialism can be considered as a substitute for capitalism, whether any rational conduct of production activities, i.e., conduct based on economic calculation, can be accomplished under socialist conditions. The bigotry and the dogmatism of the socialists manifest themselves in the fact that they stubbornly refuse to enter into an examination of these problems. With them it is a foregone conclusion that capitalism is the worst of all evils and socialism the incarnation of everything that is good. Every attempt to analyze the economic problems of a socialist commonwealth is considered as a crime of *lèse majesté*. As the conditions prevailing in the Western countries do not yet permit the liquidation of such offenders in the Russian way, they insult and vilify them, cast suspicion upon their motives and boycott them.[12]

Second: There is no economic difference between socialism and communism. Both terms, socialism and communism, denote the same system of society's economic organization, i.e., public control of all the means of production as distinct from private control of the means of production, namely capitalism. The two terms, socialism and communism, are synonyms. The document which all Marxian socialists consider as the unshakable foundation of their creed is called the Communist Manifesto. On the other hand, the official name of the communist Russian empire is Union of the *Socialist* Soviet Republics (U.S.S.R.).[13]

The antagonism between the present-day communist and socialist parties does not concern the ultimate goal of their policies. It refers mainly to the attitude of the Russian dictators to subjugate as many countries as possible, first of all the United States. It refers,

---

12 These last two sentences do not refer to three or four socialist authors of our time who—very late indeed and in a very unsatisfactory way—began to examine the economic problems of socialism. But they are literally true for all other socialists from the early origins of the socialist ideas down to our day.

13 About attempts of Stalin to make a spurious distinction between socialism and communism, cf. Mises, *Planned Chaos*, Irvington-on-Hudson, 1947, pp. 4446 (reprinted in the new edition of *Socialism*, Yale University Press, 1951, pp. 552-553).

furthermore, to the question of whether the realization of public control of the means of production should be achieved by constitutional methods or by a violent overthrow of the government in power.

Neither do the terms "planning" and "welfare state" as they are used in the language of economists, statesmen, politicians and all other people signify something different from the final goal of socialism and communism. Planning means that the plan of the government should be substituted for the plans of the individual citizens. It means that the entrepreneurs and capitalists should be deprived of the discretion to employ their capital according to their own designs and should be obliged to comply unconditionally with the orders issued by a central planning board or office. This amounts to the transfer of control from the entrepreneurs and capitalists to the government.

It is, therefore, a serious blunder to consider socialism, planning or the welfare state as solutions to the problem of society's economic organization which would differ from that of communism and which would have to be estimated as "less absolute" or "less radical." Socialism and planning are not antidotes for communism as many people seem to believe. A socialist is more moderate than a communist insofar as he does not hand out secret documents of his own country to Russian agents and does not plot to assassinate anticommunist bourgeois. This is, of course, a very important difference. But it has no reference whatever to the ultimate goal of political action.

Third: Capitalism and socialism are two distinct patterns of social organization. Private control of the means of production and public control are contradictory notions and not merely contrary notions. There is no such thing as a mixed economy, a system that would stand midway between capitalism and socialism. Those advocating what is erroneously believed to be a middle-of-the-road solution do not recommend a compromise between capitalism and socialism, but a third pattern which has its own particular features and must be judged according to its own merits. This third system that the economists call interventionism does not combine, as its champions claim, some of the features of capitalism with some of socialism. It is something entirely different from each of them. The economists who declare that interventionism does not attain those ends which its supporters want to attain but makes things worse—not from the economists' own point of view, but from the very point of view of the advocates of interventionism—are not intransigent and extremists. They merely describe the inevitable consequences of interventionism.

When Marx and Engels in the Communist Manifesto advocated definite interventionist measures, they did not mean to recommend a compromise between socialism and capitalism. They considered these measures—incidentally, the same measures which are today the essence of the New Deal and Fair Deal policies—as first steps on the way toward the establishment of full communism. They themselves described these measures as "economically insufficient and untenable," and they asked for them only because they "in the course of the movement outstrip themselves, necessitate further inroads upon the old social order, and are unavoidable as a means of entirely revolutionizing the mode of production."

Thus the social and economic philosophy of the progressives is a plea for socialism and communism.

6. The "Social" Novels and Plays

The public, committed to socialist ideas, asks for socialist ("social") novels and plays. The authors, themselves imbued with socialist ideas, are ready to deliver the stuff required. They describe unsatisfactory conditions which, as they insinuate, are the inevitable consequence of capitalism. They depict the poverty and destitution, the ignorance, dirt and disease of the exploited classes. They castigate the luxury, the stupidity and the moral corruption of the exploiting classes. In their eyes everything that is bad and ridiculous is bourgeois, and everything that is good and sublime is proletarian.

The authors who deal with the lives of the poverty-stricken can be divided into two classes. The first class are those who themselves did not experience poverty, who were born and brought up in a "bourgeois" milieu or in a milieu of prosperous wage earners or peasants and to whom the environment in which they place the characters of their plays and novels is strange. These authors must, before they start writing, collect information about the life in the underworld they want to paint. They embark upon research. But, of course, they do not approach the subject of their studies with an unbiased mind. They know beforehand what they will discover. They are convinced that the conditions of the wage earners are desolate and horrible beyond any imagination. They shut their eyes to all things they do not want to see, and find only what confirms their preconceived opinions. They have been taught by the socialists that capitalism is a system to make the masses suffer terribly and that the more capitalism progresses and approaches its full maturity, the more the immense majority becomes impoverished. Their novels and plays are designed as case studies for the demonstration of this Marxian dogma.

What is wrong with these authors is not that they choose to portray misery and destitution. An artist may display his mastership in the treatment of any kind of subject. Their blunder consists rather in the tendentious misrepresentation and misinterpretation of social conditions. They fail to realize that the shocking circumstances they describe are the outcome of the absence of capitalism, the remnants of the precapitalistic past or the effects of policies sabotaging the operation of capitalism. They do not comprehend that capitalism, in engendering big-scale production for mass consumption, is essentially a system of wiping out penury as much as possible.

They describe the wage earner only in his capacity as a factory hand and never give a thought to the fact that he is also the main consumer either of the manufactured goods themselves or of the foodstuffs and raw materials exchanged against them.

The predilection of these authors for dealing with desolation and distress turns into a scandalous distortion of truth when they imply that what they report is the state of affairs typical and representative of capitalism. The information provided by the statistical data concerning the production and the sale of all articles of big-scale production clearly shows that the typical wage earner does not live in the depths of misery.

The outstanding figure in the school of "social" literature was Émile Zola. He set the pattern which hosts of less gifted imitators adopted. In his opinion art was closely related to science. It had to be founded on research and to illustrate the findings of science. And the main result of social science, as Zola saw it, was the dogma that capitalism is the worst of all evils and that the coming of socialism is both inevitable and highly desirable. His novels were "in effect a body of socialist homiletics."[14] But Zola was, in his prosocialist bias and zeal, very soon surpassed by the "proletarian" literature of his adepts.

The "proletarian" critics of literature pretend that what these "proletarian" authors deal with is simply the unadulterated facts of proletarian experience.[15] However, these authors do not merely report facts. They interpret these facts from the point of view of the teachings of Marx, Veblen and the Webbs. This interpretation is the gist of their writings, the salient point that characterizes them as pro-socialist propaganda. These writers take the dogmas on which their explanation of events is based as self-understood and irrefutable and are fully convinced that their readers share their confidence. Thus it seems to them often superfluous to mention the doctrines

[14] Cf. P. Martino in the "*Encyclopaedia of the Social Sciences*," Vol. XV, p. 537.

[15] Cf. J. Freeman, Introduction to *Proletarian Literature in the United States, an Anthology*, New York, 1935, pp. 9-28.

explicitly. They sometimes refer to them only by implication. But this does not alter the fact that everything they convey in their books depends on the validity of the socialist tenets and pseudoeconomic constructions. Their fiction is an illustration of the lessons of the anticapitalistic doctrinaires and collapses with them.

The second class of authors of "proletarian" fiction are those who were born in the proletarian milieu they describe in their books. These men have detached themselves from the environment of manual workers and have joined the ranks of professional people. They are not like the proletarian authors of "bourgeois" background under the necessity to embark upon special research in order to learn something about the life of the wage earners. They can draw from their own experience.

This personal experience teaches them things that flatly contradict essential dogmas of the socialist creed. Gifted and hard-working sons of parents living in modest conditions are not barred from access to more satisfactory positions. The authors of "proletarian" background stand themselves in witness of this fact. They know why they themselves succeeded while most of their brothers and mates did not. In the course of their advance to a better station in life they had ample opportunity to meet other young men who, like themselves, were eager to learn and to advance. They know why some of them found their way and others missed it. Now, living with the "bourgeois," they discover that what distinguishes the man who makes more money from another who makes less is not that the former is a scoundrel. They would not have risen above the level in which they were born if they were so stupid as not to see that many of the businessmen and professional people are self-made men who, like themselves, started poor. They cannot fail to realize that differences in income are due to factors other than to those suggested by socialist resentment.

If such authors indulge in writing what is in fact pro-socialist homilectics, they are insincere. Their novels and plays are unveracious and therefore nothing but trash. They are far below the standards of the books of their colleagues of "bourgeois" origin who at least believe in what they are writing.

The socialist authors do not content themselves with depicting the conditions of the victims of capitalism. They also deal with the life and the doings of its beneficiaries, the businessmen. They are intent upon disclosing to the readers how profits come into existence. As they themselves—thank God—are not familiar with such a dirty subject, they first search for information in the books of competent historians. This is what these experts tell them about the "financial gangsters" and "robber barons" and the way they acquired riches:

> He began his career as a cattle drover, which means that he bought farmers' cattle and drove them to the market to sell. The cattle were sold to the butchers by weight. Just before they got to the market he fed them salt and gave them large quantities of water to drink. A gallon of water weighs about eight pounds. Put three or four gallons of water in a cow, and you have something extra when it comes to selling her.[16]

In this vein dozens and dozens of novels and plays report the transactions of the villain of their plot, the businessman. The tycoons became rich by selling cracked Steel and rotten food, shoes with cardboard soles and cotton goods for silk. They bribed the senators and the governors, the judges and the police. They cheated their customers and their workers. It is a very simple story.

It never occurred to these authors that their narration implicitly describes all other Americans as perfect idiots whom every rascal can easily dupe. The above-mentioned trick of the inflated cows is the most primitive and oldest method of swindling. It is hardly to be believed that there are in any part of the world cattle buyers stupid enough to be hoodwinked by it. To assume that there were

16 Cf. W. E. Woodward (*A New American History*, New York, 1938, p. 608) in narrating the biography of a businessman who endowed a Theological Seminary.

in the United States butchers who could be beguiled in this way is to expect too much from the reader's simplicity. It is the same with all similar fables.

In his private life the businessman, as the "progressive" author paints him, is a barbarian, a gambler and a drunkard. He spends his days at the race tracks, his evenings in night clubs and his nights with mistresses. As Marx and Engels pointed out in the Communist Manifesto, these "bourgeois, not content with having the wives and daughters of their proletarians at their disposal, not to speak of common prostitutes, take the greatest pleasure in seducing each other's wives." This is how American business is mirrored in a great part of American literature.[17]

17 Cf., the brilliant analysis by John Chamberlain, *The Businessman in Fiction* (Fortune, November 1948, pp. 134-148.)

IV.
The Noneconomic Objections to Capitalism

1. The Argument of Happiness

Critics level two charges against capitalism: First, they say, that the possession of a motor car, a television set and a refrigerator does not make a man happy. Secondly, they add, that there are still people who own none of these gadgets. Both propositions are correct, but they do not cast blame upon the capitalistic system of social cooperation.

People do not toil and trouble in order to attain perfect happiness, but in order to remove as much as possible some felt uneasiness and thus to become happier than they were before. A man who buys a television set thereby gives evidence to the effect that he thinks that the possession of this contrivance will increase his well-being and make him more content than he was without it. If it were otherwise, he would not have bought it. The task of the doctor is not to make the patient happy, but to remove his pain and to put him in better shape for the pursuit of the main concern of every living being, the fight against all factors pernicious to his life and ease.

It may be true that there are among Buddhist mendicants, living on alms in dirt and penury, some who feel perfectly happy and do not envy any nabob. However, it is a fact that for the immense majority of people such a life would appear unbearable. To them the impulse toward ceaselessly aiming at the improvement of the external conditions of existence is inwrought. Who would presume to set an Asiatic beggar as an example to the average American? One of the most remarkable achievements of capitalism is the drop in infant mortality. Who wants to deny that this phenomenon has at least removed one of the causes of many people's unhappiness?

No less absurd is the second reproach thrown upon capitalism—namely, that technological and therapeutical innovations do not benefit all people. Changes in human conditions are brought about by the pioneering of the most clever and most energetic men. They take the lead and the rest of mankind follows them little by little. The innovation is first a luxury of only a few people, until by degrees it comes into the reach of the many. It is not a sensible objection to the use of shoes or of forks that they spread only slowly and that even today millions do without them. The dainty ladies and gentlemen who first began to use soap were the harbingers of the big-scale production of soap for the common man. If those who have today the means to buy a television set were to abstain from the purchase because some people cannot afford it, they would not further, but hinder, the popularization of this contrivance.[18]

2. Materialism

Again there are grumblers who blame capitalism for what they call its mean materialism. They cannot help admitting that capitalism has the tendency to improve the material conditions of mankind.

[18] See pp. 42-43 about the inherent tendency of capitalism toward shortening the interval between the appearance of a new improvement and the moment its use becomes general.

But, they say, it has diverted men from the higher and nobler pursuits. It feeds the bodies, but it starves the souls and the minds. It has brought about a decay of the arts. Gone are the days of the great poets, painters, sculptors and architects. Our age produces merely trash.

The judgment about the merits of a work of art is entirely subjective. Some people praise what others disdain. There is no yardstick to measure the aesthetic worth of a poem or of a building. Those who are delighted by the Cathedral of Chartres and the *Meninas* of Velasquez may think that those who remain unaffected by these marvels are boors. Many students are bored to death when the school forces them to read *Hamlet*. Only people who are endowed with a spark of the artistic mentality are fit to appreciate and to enjoy the work of an artist.

Among those who make pretense to the appellation of educated men there is much hypocrisy. They put on an air of connoisseurship and feign enthusiasm for the art of the past and artists passed away long ago. They show no similar sympathy for the contemporary artist who still fights for recognition. Dissembled adoration for the old masters is with them a means to disparage and ridicule the new ones who deviate from traditional canons and create their own.

John Ruskin will be remembered—together with Carlyle, the Webbs, Bernard Shaw and some others—as one of the gravediggers of British freedom, civilization and prosperity. A wretched character in his private no less than in his public life, he glorified war and bloodshed and fanatically slandered the teachings of political economy which he did not understand. He was a bigoted detractor of the market economy and a romantic eulogist of the guilds. He paid homage to the arts of earlier centuries. But when he faced the work of a great living artist, Whistler, he dispraised it in such foul and objurgatory language that he was sued for libel and found guilty by the jury. It was the writings of Ruskin that popularized the prejudice that capitalism, apart from being a bad economic system, has substituted ugliness for beauty, pettiness for grandeur, trash for art.

As people widely disagree in the appreciation of artistic achievements, it is not possible to explode the talk about the artistic inferiority of the age of capitalism in the same apodictic way in which one may refute errors in logical reasoning or in the establishment of facts of experience. Yet no sane man would be insolent enough as to belittle the grandeur of the artistic exploits of the age of capitalism.

The pre-eminent art of this age of "mean materialism and money-making" was music. Wagner and Verdi, Berlioz and Bizet, Brahms and Bruckner, Hugo Wolf and Mahler, Puccini and Richard Strauss, what an illustrious cavalcade! What an era in which such masters as Schumann and Donizetti were overshadowed by still superior genius!

Then there were the great novels of Balzac, Flaubert, Maupassant, Jens Jacobsen, Proust, and the poems of Victor Hugo, Walt Whitman, Rilke, Yeats. How poor our lives would be if we had to miss the work of these giants and of many other no less sublime authors.

Let us not forget the French painters and sculptors who taught us new ways of looking at the world and enjoying light and color.

Nobody ever contested that this age has encouraged all branches of scientific activities. But, say the grumblers, this was mainly the work of specialists while "synthesis" was lacking. One can hardly misconstrue in a more absurd way the teachings of modern mathematics, physics and biology. And what about the books of philosophers like Croce, Bergson, Husserl and Whitehead?

Each epoch has its own character in its artistic exploits. Imitation of masterworks of the past is not art; it is routine. What gives value to a work is those features in which it differs from other works. This is what is called the style of a period.

In one respect the eulogists of the past seem to be justified. The last generations did not bequeath to the future such monuments as the pyramids, the Greek temples, the Gothic cathedrals and the churches and palaces of the Renaissance and the Barroco. In the last hundred years many churches and even cathedrals were built and many more government palaces, schools and libraries. But they do not show any original conception; they reflect old styles or hybridize divers old styles. Only in apartment houses, office buildings and private homes have we seen something develop that may be qualified as an architectural style of our age. Although it would be mere pedantry not to appreciate the peculiar grandeur of such sights as the New York skyline, it can be admitted that modern architecture has not attained the distinction of that of past centuries.

The reasons are various. As far as religious buildings are concerned, the accentuated conservatism of the churches shuns any innovation. With the passing of dynasties and aristocracies, the impulse to construct new palaces disappeared. The wealth of entrepreneurs and capitalists is, whatever the anticapitalistic demagogues may fable, so much inferior to that of kings and princes that they cannot indulge in such luxurious construction. No one is today rich enough to plan such palaces as that of Versailles or the Escorial. The orders for the construction of government buildings do no longer emanate from despots who were free, in defiance of public opinion, to choose a master whom they themselves held in esteem and to sponsor a project that scandalized the dull majority. Committees and councils are not likely to adopt the ideas of bold pioneers. They prefer to range themselves on the safe side.

There has never been an era in which the many were prepared to do justice to contemporary art. Reverence to the great authors and artists has always been limited to small groups. What characterizes capitalism is not the bad taste of the crowds, but the fact that these crowds, made prosperous by capitalism, became "consumers" of literature—of course, of trashy literature. The book market is flooded by a downpour of trivial fiction for the semibarbarians. But this does not prevent great authors from creating imperishable works.

The critics shed tears on the alleged decay of the industrial arts. They contrast, e.g., old furniture as preserved in the castles of European aristocratic families and in the collections of the museums with the cheap things turned out by big-scale production. They fail to see that these collectors' items were made exclusively for the well-to-do. The carved chests and the intarsia tables could not be found in the miserable huts of the poorer strata. Those caviling about the inexpensive furniture of the American wage earner should cross the Rio Grande del Norte and inspect the abodes of the Mexican peons which are devoid of any furniture. When modern industry began to provide the masses with the paraphernalia of a better life, their main concern was to produce as cheaply as possible without any regard to aesthetic values. Later, when the progress of capitalism had raised the masses' standard of living, they turned step by step to the fabrication of things which do not lack refinement and beauty. Only romantic prepossession can induce an observer to ignore the fact that more and more citizens of the capitalistic countries live in an environment which cannot be simply dismissed as ugly.

3. *Injustice*

The most passionate detractors of capitalism are those who reject it on account of its alleged injustice.

It is a gratuitous pastime to depict what *ought* to be and is not because it is contrary to inflexible laws of the real universe. Such reveries may be considered as innocuous as long as they remain daydreams. But when their authors begin to ignore the difference between fantasy and reality, they become the most serious obstacle to human endeavors to improve the external conditions of life and well-being.

The worst of all these delusions is the idea that "nature" has bestowed upon every man certain rights. According to this doctrine nature is openhanded toward every child born. There is plenty of everything for everybody. Consequently, everyone has a fair inalienable claim against all his fellow men and against society that he should get the full portion which nature has allotted to him. The eternal laws of natural and divine justice require that nobody should appropriate to himself what by rights belongs to other people. The poor are needy only because unjust people have deprived them of their birthright. It is the task of the church and the secular authorities to prevent such spoliation and to make all people prosperous.

Every word of this doctrine is false. Nature is not bountiful but stingy. It has restricted the supply of all things indispensable for the preservation of human life. It has populated the world with animals and plants to whom the impulse to destroy human life and welfare is inwrought. It displays powers and elements whose operation is damaging to human life and to human endeavors to preserve it. Man's survival and well-being are an achievement of the skill with which he has utilized the main instrument with which nature has equipped him—reason. Men, cooperating under the system of the division of labor, have created all the wealth which the daydreamers consider as a free gift of nature. With regard to the "distribution" of this wealth, it is non-sensical to refer to an allegedly divine or natural principle of justice. What matters is not the allocation of portions out of a fund presented to man by nature. The problem is rather to further those social institutions which enable people to continue and to enlarge the production of all those things which they need.

The World Council of Churches, an ecumenical organization of Protestant Churches, declared in 1948: "Justice demands that the inhabitants of Asia and Africa, for instance, should have the benefits of more machine production."[19] This makes sense only if one

[19] Cf. *The Church and the Disorder of Society*, New York, 1948, p. 198.

implies that the Lord presented mankind with a definite quantity of machines and expected that these contrivances will be distributed equally among the various nations. Yet the capitalistic countries were bad enough to take possession of much more of this stock than "justice" would have assigned to them and thus to deprive the inhabitants of Asia and Africa of their fair portion. What a shame!

The truth is that the accumulation of capital and its investment in machines, the source of the comparatively greater wealth of the Western peoples, are due exclusively to laissez-faire capitalism which the same document of the Churches passionately misrepresents and rejects on moral grounds. It is not the fault of the capitalists that the Asiatics and Africans did not adopt those ideologies and policies which would have made the evolution of autochthonous capitalism possible. Neither is it the fault of the capitalists that the policies of these nations thwarted the attempts of foreign investors to give them "the benefits of more machine production." No one contests that what makes hundreds of millions in Asia and Africa destitute is that they cling to primitive methods of production and miss the benefits which the employment of better tools and up-to-date technological designs could bestow upon them. But there is only one means to relieve their distress—namely, the full adoption of laissez-faire capitalism. What they need is private enterprise and the accumulation of new capital, capitalists and entrepreneurs. It is nonsensical to blame capitalism and the capitalistic nations of the West for the plight the backward peoples have brought upon themselves. The remedy indicated is not "justice" but the substitution of sound, i.e., laissez-faire, policies for unsound policies.

It was not vain disquisitions about a vague concept of justice that raised the standard of living of the common man in the capitalistic countries to its present height, but the activities of men dubbed as "rugged individualists" and "exploiters." The poverty of the backward nations is due to the fact that their policies of expropriation, discriminatory taxation and foreign exchange control prevent the investment of foreign capital while their domestic policies preclude the accumulation of indigenous capital.

All those rejecting capitalism on moral grounds as an unfair system are deluded by their failure to comprehend what capital is, how it comes into existence and how it is maintained, and what the benefits are which are derived from its employment in production processes.

The only source of the generation of additional capital goods is saving. If all the goods produced are consumed, no new capital comes into being. But if consumption lags behind production and the surplus of goods newly produced over goods consumed is utilized in further production processes, these processes are henceforth carried out by the aid of more capital goods. All the capital goods are intermediary goods, stages on the road that leads from the first employment of the original factors of production, i.e., natural resources and human labor, to the final turning out of goods ready for consumption. They all are perishable. They are, sooner or later, worn out in the processes of production. If all the products are consumed without replacement of the capital goods which have been used up in their production, capital is consumed. If this happens, further production will be aided only by a smaller amount of capital goods and will therefore render a smaller output per unit of the natural resources and labor employed. To prevent this sort of dissaving and disinvestment, one must dedicate a part of the productive effort to capital maintenance, to the replacement of the capital goods absorbed in the production of usable goods.

Capital is not a free gift of God or of nature. It is the outcome of a provident restriction of consumption on the part of man. It is created and increased by saving and maintained by the abstention from dissaving.

Neither have capital or capital goods in themselves the power to raise the productivity of natural resources and of human labor. Only if the fruits of saving are wisely employed or invested, do they increase the output per unit of the input of natural resources and of labor. If this is not the case, they are dissipated or wasted.

The accumulation of new capital, the maintenance of previously accumulated capital and the utilization of capital for raising the productivity of human effort are the fruits of purposive human action. They are the outcome of the conduct of thrifty people who save and abstain from dissaving, viz., the capitalists who earn interest; and of people who succeed in utilizing the capital available for the best possible satisfaction of the needs of the consumers, viz., the enterpreneurs who earn profit.

Neither capital (or capital goods) nor the conduct of the capitalists and entrepreneurs in dealing with capital could improve the standard of living for the rest of the people, if these noncapitalists and nonentrepreneurs did not react in a certain way. If the wage earners were to behave in the way which the spurious "iron law of wages" describes and would know of no use for their earnings other than to feed and to procreate more offspring, the increase in capital accumulated would keep pace with the increase in population figures. All the benefits derived from the accumulation of additional capital would be absorbed by multiplying the number of people. However, men do not respond to an improvement in the external conditions of their lives in the way in which rodents and germs do. They know also of other satisfactions than feeding and proliferation. Consequently, in the countries of capitalistic civilization, the increase of capital accumulated outruns the increase in population figures. To the extent that this happens, the marginal productivity of labor is increased as against the marginal productivity of the material factors of production. There emerges a tendency toward higher wage rates. The proportion of the total output of production that goes to the wage earners is enhanced as against that which goes as interest to the capitalists and as rent to the land owners.[20]

20 Profits are not affected. They are the gain derived from adjusting the employment of material factors of production and of labor to changes occurring in demand and supply and solely depend on the size of the previous maladjustment and the degree of its removal. They are transient and

To speak of the productivity of labor makes sense only if one refers to the marginal productivity of labor, i.e., to the deduction in net output to be caused by the elimination of one worker. Then it refers to a definite economic quantity, to a determinate amount of goods or its equivalent in money. The concept of a general productivity of labor as resorted to in popular talk about an allegedly natural right of the workers to claim the total increase in productivity is empty and indefinable. It is based on the illusion that it is possible to determine the shares that each of the various complementary factors of production has physically contributed to the turning out of the product. If one cuts a sheet of paper with scissors, it is impossible to ascertain quotas of the outcome to the scissors (or to each of the two blades) and to the man who handled them. To manufacture a car one needs various machines and tools, various raw materials, the labor of various manual workers and, first of all, the plan of a designer. But nobody can decide what quota of the finished car is to be physically ascribed to each of the various factors the cooperation of which was required for the production of the car.

For the sake of argument, we may for a moment set aside all the considerations which show the fallacies of the popular treatment of the problem and ask: Which of the two factors, labor or capital, caused the increase in productivity? But precisely if we put the question in this way, the answer must be: capital. What renders the total output in the present-day United States higher (per head of manpower employed) than output in earlier ages or in economically backward countries—for instance, China—is the fact that the contemporary American worker is aided by more and better tools. If capital equipment (per head of the worker) were not more abundant than it was three hundred years ago or than it is today in China, output (per head of the worker) would not be higher. What is required to raise, in the absence of an increase in the number of

disappear once the maladjustment has been entirely removed. But as changes in demand and supply again and again occur, new sources of profit emerge also again and again.

workers employed, the total amount of America's industrial output is the investment of additional capital that can only be accumulated by new saving. It is those saving and investing to whom credit is to be given for the multiplication of the productivity of the total labor force.

What raises wage rates and allots to the wage earners an ever increasing portion out of the output which has been enhanced by additional capital accumulation is the fact that the rate of capital accumulation exceeds the rate of increase in population. The official doctrine passes over this fact in silence or even denies it emphatically. But the policies of the unions clearly show that their leaders are fully aware of the correctness of the theory which they publicly smear as silly bourgeois apologetics. They are eager to restrict the number of job seekers in the whole country by anti-immigration laws and in each segment of the labor market by preventing the influx of newcomers.

That the increase in wage rates does not depend on the individual worker's "productivity," but on the marginal productivity of labor, is clearly demonstrated by the fact that wage rates are moving upward also for performances in which the "productivity" of the individual has not changed at all. There are many such jobs. A barber shaves a customer today precisely in the same manner his predecessors used to shave people two hundred years ago. A butler waits at the table of the British prime minister in the same way in which once butlers served Pitt and Palmerston. In agriculture some kinds of work are still performed with the same tools in the same way in which they were performed centuries ago. Yet the wage rates earned by all such workers are today much higher than they were in the past. They are higher because they are determined by the marginal productivity of labor. The employer of a butler withholds this man from employment in a factory and must therefore pay the equivalent of the increase in output which the additional employment of one man in a factory would bring about. It is not any merit on the part of the butler that causes this rise in his wages, but the fact that the increase in capital invested surpasses the increase in the number of hands.

All pseudo-economic doctrines which depreciate the role of saving and capital accumulation are absurd. What constitutes the greater wealth of a capitalistic society as against the smaller wealth of a noncapitalistic society is the fact that the available supply of capital goods is greater in the former than in the latter. What has improved the wage earners' standard of living is the fact that the capital equipment per head of the men eager to earn wages has increased. It is a consequence of this fact that an ever increasing portion of the total amount of usable goods produced goes to the wage earners. None of the passionate tirades of Marx, Keynes and a host of less well known authors could show a weak point in the statement that there is only one means to raise wage rates permanently and for the benefit of all those eager to earn wages—namely, to accelerate the increase in capital available as against population. If this be "unjust," then the blame rests with nature and not with man.

4. The "Bourgeois Prejudice" for Liberty

The history of Western civilization is the record of a ceaseless struggle for liberty.

Social cooperation under the division of labor is the ultimate and sole source of man's success in his struggle for survival and his endeavors to improve as much as possible the material conditions of his well-being. But as human nature is, society cannot exist if there is no provision for preventing unruly people from actions incompatible with community life. In order to preserve peaceful cooperation, one must be ready to resort to violent suppression of those disturbing the peace. Society cannot do without a social apparatus of coercion and compulsion, i.e., without state and government. Then a further problem emerges: to restrain the men who are in charge of the governmental functions lest they abuse their power and convert all other people into virtual slaves. The aim of all struggles for liberty is to keep in bounds the armed defenders of peace, the governors and their constables. The political concept of the individual's freedom means: freedom from arbitrary action on the part of the police power.

The idea of liberty is and has always been peculiar to the West. What separates East and West is first of all the fact that the peoples of the East never conceived the idea of liberty. The imperishable glory of the ancient Greeks was that they were the first to grasp the meaning and significance of institutions warranting liberty. Recent historical research has traced back the origin of some of the scientific achievements previously credited to the Hellenes to oriental sources. But nobody has ever contested that the idea of liberty originated in the cities of ancient Greece. The writings of Greek philosophers and historians transmitted it to the Romans and later to modern Europe and America. It became the essential concern of all Western plans for the establishment of the good society. It begot the laissez-faire philosophy to which mankind owes all the unprecedented achievements of the age of capitalism.

The purpose of all modern political and judicial institutions is to safeguard the individuals' freedom against encroachments on the part of the government. Representative government and the rule of law, the independence of courts and tribunals from interference on the part of administrative agencies, habeas corpus, judicial examination and redress of acts of the administration, freedom of speech and the press, separation of state and church, and many other institutions aimed at one end only: to restrain the discretion of the officeholders and to render the individuals free from their arbitrariness. The age of capitalism has abolished all vestiges of slavery and serfdom. It has put an end to cruel punishments and has reduced the penalty for crimes committed to the minimum indispensable for discouraging offenders. It has done away with torture and other objectionable methods of dealing with suspects and law breakers. It has repealed all privileges and promulgated equality o£ all men under the law. It has transformed the subjects of tyranny into free citizens.

The material improvements were the fruit of these reforms and innovations in the conduct of government affairs. As all privileges disappeared and everybody was granted the right to challenge the vested interests of all other people, a free hand was given to those who had the ingenuity to develop all the new industries which today render the material conditions of people more satisfactory. Population figures multiplied and yet the increased population could enjoy a better life than their ancestors.

Also in the countries of Western civilization there have always been advocates of tyranny—the absolute arbitrary rule of an autocrat or of an aristocracy on the one hand, and the subjection of all other people on the other hand. But in the age of Enlightenment these voices became thinner and thinner. The cause of liberty prevailed. In the first part of the nineteenth century the victorious advance of the principle of freedom seemed to be irresistible. The most eminent philosophers and historians got the conviction that historical evolution tends toward the establishment of institutions warranting freedom and that no intrigues and machinations on the part of the champions of servilism could stop the trend toward liberalism.

In dealing with the liberal social philosophy there is a disposition to overlook the power of an important factor that worked in favor of the idea of liberty, viz., the eminent role assigned to the literature of ancient Greece in the education of the élite. There were among the Greek authors also champions of government omnipotence, such as Plato. But the essential tenor of Greek ideology was the pursuit of liberty. Judged by the standards of modern institutions, the Greek city-states must be called oligarchies. The liberty which the Greek statesmen, philosophers and historians glorified as the most precious good of man was a privilege reserved to a minority. In denying it to metics and slaves they virtually advocated the despotic rule of a hereditary caste of oligarchs. Yet it would be a grave error to dismiss their hymns to liberty as mendacious. They were no less sincere in their praise and quest of freedom than were, two thousand years later, the slave-holders among the signers of the American Declaration of Independence. It was the political literature of the ancient Greeks that begot the ideas of the Monarchomachs, the philosophy of the Whigs, the doctrines of Althusius, Grotius and John Locke and the ideology of the fathers of modern constitutions and bills of rights. It was the classical studies, the essential feature of a liberal education, that kept awake the spirit of freedom in the England of the Stuarts, in the France of the Bourbons, and in Italy subject to the despotism of a galaxy of princes. No less a man than Bismarck, among the nineteenth-century statesmen next to Metternich the foremost foe of liberty, bears witness to the fact that, even in the Prussia of Frederick William III, the *Gymnasium*, the education based on Greek and Roman literature, was a stronghold of republicanism.[21] The passionate endeavors to eliminate the classical studies from the curriculum of the liberal education and thus virtually to destroy its very character were one of the major manifestations of the revival of the servile ideology.

It is a fact that a hundred years ago only a few people anticipated the over-powering momentum which the antilibertarian ideas were destined to acquire in a very short time. The ideal of liberty seemed to be so firmly rooted that everybody thought that no reactionary movement could ever succeed in eradicating it. It is true, it would have been a hopeless venture to attack freedom openly and to advocate unfeignedly a return to subjection and bondage. But antiliberalism got hold of peoples' minds camouflaged as super-liberalism, as the fulfillment and consummation of the

21 Cf. Bismarck, *Gedankjen und Erinnerungcn*, New York, 1898, Vol. I, p. 1.

very ideas of freedom and liberty. It came disguised as socialism, communism, planning.

No intelligent man could fail to recognize that what the socialists, communists and planners were aiming at was the most radical abolition of the individuals' freedom and the establishment of government omnipotence. Yet the immense majority of the socialist intellectuals were convinced that in fighting for socialism they were fighting for freedom. They called themselves left-wingers and democrats, and nowadays they are even claiming for themselves the epithet "liberal."

We have already dealt with the psychological factors that dimmed the judgment of these intellectuals and the masses who followed their lead. They were in their subconsciousness fully aware of the fact that their failure to attain the far-flung goals which their ambition impelled them to aim at was due to deficiencies of their own. They knew very well that they were either not bright enough or not industrious enough. But they were eager not to avow their inferiority both to themselves and to their fellow men and to search for a scapegoat. They consoled themselves and tried to convince other people that the cause of their failure was not their own inferiority but the injustice of society's economic organization. Under capitalism, they declared, self-realization is only possible for the few. "Liberty in a laissez-faire society is attainable only by those who have the wealth or opportunity to purchase it."[22] Hence, they concluded, the state must interfere in order to realize "social justice"—what they really meant was, in order to give to the frustrated mediocrity "according to his needs."

As long as the problems of socialism were merely a matter of debates, people who lack clear judgment and understanding could fall prey to the illusion that freedom could be preserved under a socialist regime. Such self-deceit can no longer be nurtured since the Soviet experience has shown to everybody what conditions are

[22] Cf. H. Laski, article *Liberty* in the *Encyclopaedia of the Social Sciences*, IX, p. 443.

in a socialist commonwealth. Today the apologists of socialism are forced to distort facts and to misrepresent the manifest meaning of words when they want to make people believe in the compatibility of socialism and freedom.

The late Professor Laski—in his lifetime an eminent member and chairman of the British Labour Party, a self-styled noncommunist or even anticommunist—told us that "no doubt in Soviet Russia a Communist has a full sense of liberty; no doubt also he has a keen sense that liberty is denied him in Fascist Italy."[23] The truth is that a Russian is free to obey all the orders issued by his superiors. But as soon as he deviates a hundredth of an inch from the correct way of thinking as laid down by the authorities, he is mercilessly liquidated. All those politicians, officeholders, authors, musicians and scientists who were "purged" were—to be sure—not anticommunists. They were, on the contrary, fanatical communists, party members in good standing, whom the supreme authorities, in due recognition of their loyalty to the Soviet creed, had promoted to high positions. The only offense they had committed was that they were not quick enough in adjusting their ideas, policies, books or compositions to the latest changes in the ideas and tastes of Stalin. It is difficult to believe that these people had "a full sense of liberty" if one does not attach to the word *liberty* a sense which is precisely the contrary of the sense which all people always used to attach to it.

Fascist Italy was certainly a country in which there was no liberty. It had adopted the notorious Soviet pattern of the "one party principle" and accordingly suppressed all dissenting views. Yet there was still a conspicuous difference between the Bolshevik and the Fascist application of this principle. For instance, there lived in Fascist Italy a former member of the parliamentary group of communist deputies, who remained loyal unto death to his communist tenets, Professor Antonio Graziadei. He received the government pension which he was entitled to claim as professor emeritus, and

23 Cf. Laski, l.c., pp. 445-446.

he was free to write and to publish, with the most eminent Italian publishing firms, books which were orthodox Marxian. His lack of liberty was certainly less rigid than that of the Russian communists who, as Professor Laski chose to say, "no doubt" have "a full sense of liberty."

Professor Laski took pleasure in repeating the truism that liberty in practice always means liberty within law. He goes on saying that the law always aims at "the conference of security upon a way of life which is deemed satisfactory by those who dominate the machinery of State."[24] This is a correct description of the laws of a free country if it means that the law aims at protecting society against conspiracies intent upon kindling civil war and upon overthrowing the government by violence. But it is a serious misstatement when Professor Laski adds that in a capitalistic society "an effort on the part of the poor to alter in a radical way the property rights of the rich at once throws the whole scheme of liberties into jeopardy."[25]

Take the case of the great idol of Professor Laski and all his friends, Karl Marx. When in 1848 and 1849 he took an active part in the organization and the conduct of the revolution, first in Prussia and later also in other German States, he was—being legally an alien—expelled and moved, with his wife, his children and his maid, first to Paris and then to London.[26] Later, when peace returned and the abettors of the abortive revolution were amnestied, he was free to return to all parts of Germany and often made use of this opportunity. He was no longer an exile, and he chose of his own accord to make his home in London.[27] Nobody molested him when he founded, in 1864, the International Working Men's

---

24 Cf. Laski, l.c., p. 446.

25 Cf. Laski, l.c., p. 446.

26 About Marx's activities in the years 1848 and 1849 see: *Karl Marx, Chronik seines Lebens in Einzeldaten,* published by the Marx-Engels-Lenin-Institut in Moskau, 1934, pp. 43-81.

27 In 1845 Marx *voluntarily* of his own accord renounced his Prussian citizenship. When later, in the early sixties, he considered a political career in Prussia, the government denied his application for restoring his citizenship. Thus, a political career was closed to him. Perhaps this fact decided him to remain in London.

Association, a body whose avowed sole purpose was to prepare the great world revolution. He was not stopped when, on behalf of this association, he visited various continental countries. He was free to write and to publish books and articles which, to use the words of Professor Laski, were certainly an effort "to alter in a radical way the property rights of the rich." And he died quietly in his London home, 41 Maitland Park Road, on March 14, 1883.

Or take the case of the British Labour Party. Their effort "to alter in a radical way the property rights of the rich" was, as Professor Laski knew very well, not hindered by any action incompatible with the principle of liberty.

Marx, the dissenter, could live, write and advocate revolution, at ease, in Victorian England just as the Labour Party could engage in all political activities, at ease, in post-Victorian England. In Soviet Russia not the slightest opposition is tolerated. This is the difference between liberty and slavery.

5. *Liberty and Western Civilization*

The critics of the legal and constitutional concept of liberty and the institutions devised for its practical realization are right in their assertion that freedom from arbitrary action on the part of the officeholders is in itself not yet sufficient to make an individual free. But in emphasizing this indisputable truth they are running against open doors. For no advocate of liberty ever contended that to restrain the arbitrariness of officialdom is all that is needed to make the citizens free. What gives to the individuals as much freedom as is compatible with life in society is the operation of the market economy. The constitutions and bills of rights do not create freedom. They merely protect the freedom that the competitive economic system grants to the individuals against encroachments on the part of the police power.

In the market economy people have the opportunity to strive after the station they want to attain in the structure of the social division of labor. They are free to choose the vocation in which they plan to serve their fellow men. In a planned economy they lack this right. Here the authorities determine each man's occupation. The discretion of the superiors promotes a man to a better position or denies him such promotion. The individual depends entirely on the good graces of those in power. But under capitalism everybody is free to challenge the vested interests of everybody else. If he thinks that he has the ability to supply the public better or more cheaply than other people do, he may try to demonstrate his efficiency. Lack of funds cannot frustrate his projects. For the capitalists are always in search of men who can utilize their funds in the most profitable way. The outcome of a man's business activities depends alone on the conduct of the consumers who buy what they like best.

Neither does the wage earner depend on the employer's arbitrariness. An entrepreneuer who fails to hire those workers who are best fitted for the job concerned and to pay them enough to prevent them from taking another job is penalized by a reduction of net revenue. The employer does not grant to his employees a favor. He hires them as an indispensable means for the success of his business in the same way in which he buys raw materials and factory equipment. The worker is free to find the employment which suits him best.

The process of social selection that determines each individual's position and income is continuously going on in the market economy. Great fortunes are shrinking and finally melting away completely while other people, born in poverty, ascend to eminent positions and considerable incomes. Where there are no privileges and where governments do not grant protection to vested interests threatened by the superior efficiency of newcomers, those who have acquired wealth in the past are forced to acquire it every day anew in competition with all other people.

Within the framework of social cooperation under the division of labor everybody depends on the recognition of his services on the part of the buying public of which he himself is a member. Everybody in buying or abstaining from buying is a member of the supreme court which assigns to all people—and thereby also to himself—a definite place in society. Everybody is instrumental in the process that assigns to some people a higher, and to others a smaller, income. Everybody is free to make a contribution which his fellow men are prepared to reward by the allocation of a higher income. Freedom under capitalism means: not to depend more on other people's discretion than these others depend on one's own. No other freedom is conceivable where production is performed under the division of labor, and there is no perfect economic autarky of everybody.

There is no need to stress the point that the essential argument advanced in favor of capitalism and against socialism is not the fact that socialism must necessarily abolish all vestiges of freedom and convert all people into slaves of those in power. Socialism is unrealizable as an economic system because a socialist society would not have any possibility of resorting to economic calculation. This is why it cannot be considered as a system of society's economic organization. It is a means to disintegrate social cooperation and to bring about poverty and chaos.

In dealing with the liberty issue one does not refer to the essential economic problem of the antagonism between capitalism and socialism. One rather points out that Western man as different from the Asiatics is entirely a being adjusted to life in freedom and formed by life in freedom. The civilizations of China, Japan, India and the Mohammedan countries of the near East as they existed before these nations became acquainted with Western ways of life certainly cannot be dismissed as barbarism. These peoples, already many hundreds, even thousands of years ago, brought about marvelous achievements in the industrial arts, in architecture, in literature and philosophy and in the development of educational institutions. They founded and organized powerful empires. But then their effort was arrested, their cultures became numb and torpid, and they lost the ability to cope successfully with economic problems. Their intellectual and artistic genius withered away. Their artists and authors bluntly copied traditional patterns. Their theologians, philosophers and lawyers indulged in unvarying exegesis of old works. The monuments erected by their ancestors crumbled. Their empires disintegrated. Their citizens lost vigor and energy and became apathetic in the face of progressing decay and impoverishment.

The ancient works of oriental philosophy and poetry can compare with the most valuable works of the West. But for many centuries the East has not generated any book of importance. The intellectual and literary history of modern ages hardly records any name of an oriental author. The East has no longer contributed anything to the intellectual effort of mankind. The problems and controversies that agitated the West remained unknown to the East. In Europe there was commotion; in the East there was stagnation, indolence and indifference.

The reason is obvious. The East lacked the primordial thing, the idea of freedom from the state. The East never raised the banner of freedom, it never tried to stress the rights of the individual against the power of the rulers. It never called into question the arbitrariness of the despots. And, consequently, it never established the legal framework that would protect the private citizens' wealth against confiscation on the part of the tyrants. On the contrary, deluded by the idea that the wealth of the rich is the cause of the poverty of the poor, all people approved of the practice of the governors of expropriating successful businessmen. Thus big-scale capital accumulation was prevented, and the nations had to miss all those improvements that require considerable investment of capital. No "bourgeoisie" could develop, and consequently there was no public to encourage and to patronize authors, artists and inventors. To the sons of the people all roads toward personal distinction were closed but one. They could try to make their way in serving the princes. Western society was a community of individuals who could compete for the highest prizes. Eastern society was an agglomeration of subjects entirely dependent on the good graces of the sovereigns. The alert youth of the West looks upon the world as a field of action in which he can win fame, eminence, honors and wealth; nothing appears too difficult for his ambition. The meek progeny of Eastern parents know of nothing else than to follow the routine of their environment. The noble self-reliance of Western man found triumphant expression in such dithyrambs as Sophocles' choric Antigone-hymn upon man and his enterprising effort and Beethoven's Ninth Symphony. Nothing of the kind has been ever heard in the Orient.

Is it possible that the scions of the builders of the white man's civilization should renounce their freedom and voluntarily surrender to the suzerainty of omnipotent government? That they should seek contentment in a system in which their only task will be to serve as cogs in a vast machine designed and operated by an almighty planmaker? Should the mentality of the arrested civilizations sweep the ideals for the ascendancy of which thousands and thousands have sacrificed their lives?

Ruere in servitium, they plunged into slavery, Tacitus sadly observed in speaking of the Romans of the age of Tiberius.

V.
"Anticommunism" versus Capitalism

In the universe there is never and nowhere stability and immobility. Change and transformation are essential features of life. Each state of affairs is transient; each age is an age of transition. In human life there is never calm and repose. Life is a process, not a perseverance in a *status quo.* Yet the human mind has always been deluded by the image of an unchangeable existence. The avowed aim of all utopian movements is to put an end to history and to establish a final and permanent calm.

The psychological reasons for this tendency are obvious. Every change alters the external conditions of life and well- being and forces people to adjust themselves anew to the modification of their environments. It hurts vested interests and threatens traditional ways of production and consumption. It annoys all those who are intellectually inert and shrink from revising their modes of thinking. Conservatism is contrary to the very nature of human acting. But it has always been the cherished program of the many, of the inert who dully resist every attempt to improve their own conditions which the minority of the alert initiate. In employing the term *reactionary* one mostly refers only to the aristocrats and priests who called their parties conservative. Yet the outstanding examples of the reactionary spirit were provided by other groups: by the guilds of artisans blocking entrance into their field to newcomers; by the farmers asking for tariff protection, subsidies and "parity prices"; by the wage earners hostile to technological improvements and fostering featherbedding and similar practices.

The vain arrogance of the literati and the Bohemian artists dismisses the activities of the businessmen as unintellectual money-making. The truth is that the entrepreneurs and promoters display more intellectual faculties and intuition than the average writer and painter. The inferiority of many self-styled intellectuals manifests itself precisely in the fact that they fail to recognize what capacity and reasoning power are required to develop and to operate successfully a business enterprise.

The emergence of a numerous class of such frivolous intellectuals is one of the least welcome phenomena of the age of modern capitalism. Their obtrusive stir repels discriminating people. They are a nuisance. It would not directly harm anybody if something would be done to curb their bustle or, even better, to wipe out entirely their cliques and coteries.

However, freedom is indivisible. Every attempt to restrict the freedom of the decadent troublesome literati and pseudo-artists would vest in the authorities the power to determine what is good and what is bad. It would socialize intellectual and artistic effort. It is questionable whether it would weed out the useless and objectionable persons; but it is certain that it would put insurmountable obstacles in the way of the creative genius. The powers that be do not like new ideas, new ways of thought and new styles of art. They are opposed to any kind of innovation. Their supremacy would result in strict regimentation; it would bring about stagnation and decay.

The moral corruption, the licentiousness and the intellectual sterility of a class of lewd would-be authors and artists is the ransom mankind must pay lest the creative pioneers be prevented from accomplishing their work. Freedom must be granted to all, even to base people, lest the few who can use it for the benefit of mankind be hindered. The license which the shabby characters of the *quartier Latin* enjoyed was one of the conditions that made possible the ascendance of a few great writers, painters and sculptors. The first thing a genius needs is to breathe free air.

After all, it is not the frivolous doctrines of the Bohemians that generate disaster, but the fact that the public is ready to accept them favorably. The response to these pseudo philosophies on the part of the molders of public opinion and later on the part of the misguided masses is the evil. People are anxious to endorse the tenets they consider as fashionable lest they appear boorish and backward.

The most pernicious ideology of the last sixty years was George Sorel's syndicalism and his enthusiasm for the *action directe*. Generated by a frustrated French intellectual, it soon captivated the literati of all European countries. It was a major factor in the radicalization of all subversive movements. It influenced French royalism, militarism and anti-Semitism. It played an important role in the evolution of Russian Bolshevism, Italian Fascism and the German youth movement which finally resulted in the development of Nazism. It transformed political parties intent upon winning through electoral campaigns into factions which relied upon the organization of armed bands. It brought into discredit representative government and "bourgeois security," and preached the gospel both of civil and of foreign war. Its main slogan was: violence and again violence. The present state of European affairs is to a great extent an outcome of the prevalence of Sorel's teachings.

The intellectuals were the first to hail the ideas of Sorel; they made them popular. But the tenor of Sorelism was obviously anti-intellectual. He was opposed to cool reasoning and sober deliberation. What counts for Sorel is solely the deed, viz., the act of violence for the sake of violence. Fight for a myth whatever this myth may mean, was his advice. "If you place yourself on this ground of myths, you are proof against any kind of critical refutation."[28] What a marvelous philosophy, to destroy for the sake of destruction! Do not talk, do not reason, kill! Sorel rejects the "intellectual effort" even of the literary champions of revolution. The essential aim of the myth is "to prepare people to fight for the destruction of what exists."[29]

Yet the blame for the spread of the destructionist pseudo-philosophy rests neither with Sorel nor with his disciples, Lenin, Mussolini and Rosenberg, nor with the hosts of irresponsible literati and artists. The catastrophe came because, for many decades, hardly anybody ventured to examine critically and to explode the trigger-consciousness of the fanatical desperadoes. Even those authors who refrained from unreservedly endorsing the ideas of reckless violence were eager to find some sympathetic interpretation of the worst excesses of the dictators. The first timid objections were raised only when—very late, indeed—the intellectual abettors of these policies began to realize that even enthusiastic endorsement of the totalitarian ideology did not guarantee immunity from torture and execution.

There exists today a sham anticommunist front. What these people who call themselves "anticommunist liberals" and whom sober men more correctly call "anti-anticommunists" are aiming at is communism without those inherent and necessary features of communism which are still unpalatable to Americans. They make an illusory distinction between communism and socialism and—paradoxically enough—look for a support of their recommendation of noncommunist socialism to the document which its authors called *The Communist Manifesto.* They think that they have proved their case by employing such aliases for socialism as planning or the welfare state. They pretend to reject the revolutionary and dictatorial aspirations of the "Reds" and at the same time they praise in books and magazines, in schools and universities, Karl Marx,

[28] Cf. G. Sorel, *Réflexions sur la violence,* 3rd ed., Paris, 1912, p. 49.

[29] Cf. Sorel, l.c., p. 46.

the champion of the communist revolution and the dictatorship of the proletariat, as one of the greatest economists, philosophers and sociologists and as the eminent benefactor and liberator of mankind. They want to make us believe that untotalitarian totalitarianism, a kind of a triangular square, is the patent medicine for all ills. Whenever they raise some mild objection to communism, they are eager to abuse capitalism in terms borrowed from the objurgatory vocabulary of Marx and Lenin. They emphasize that they abhor capitalism much more passionately than communism, and they justify all the unsavory acts of the communists by referring to the "unspeakable horrors" of capitalism. In short: they pretend to fight communism in trying to convert people to the ideas of the Communist Manifesto.

What these self-styled "anticommunist liberals" are fighting against is not communism as such, but a communist in system in which they themselves are not at the helm. What they are aiming at is a socialist, i.e., communist, system in which they themselves or their most intimate friends hold the reins of government. It would perhaps be too much to say that they are burning with a desire to liquidate other people. They simply do not wish to be liquidated. In a socialist commonwealth, only the supreme autocrat and his abettors have this assurance.

An "anti-something" movement displays a purely negative attitude. It has no chance whatever to succeed. Its passionate diatribes virtually advertise the program that they attack. People must light for something that they want to achieve, not simply reject an evil, however bad it may be. They must, without any reservations, endorse the program of the market economy.

Communism would have today, after the disillusionment brought by the deeds of the Soviets and the lamentable failure of all socialist experiments, but little chance of succeeding in the West if it were not for this faked anticommunism.

What alone can prevent the civilized nations of Western Europe, America and Australia from being enslaved by the barbarism of Moscow is open and unrestricted support of laissez-faire capitalism.

Index

Made in United States
North Haven, CT
04 November 2026

21767232R00060